BUILDING
HISTORY
SERIES

THE
ROMAN
COLOSSEUM

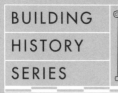

THE
ROMAN
COLOSSEUM

by Don Nardo

Lucent Books, Inc., San Diego, California

Library of Congress Cataloging-in-Publication Data

Nardo, Don, 1947–
    The Roman Colosseum / by Don Nardo.
        p.   cm. — (Building history series)
    Includes bibliographical references and index.
    Summary: Describes the planning and construction of the
Colosseum in ancient Rome and traces its history through subsequent centuries.
    ISBN 1-56006-429-3 (alk. paper)
    1. Colosseum (Rome, Italy)—Design and construction—
Juvenile literature.   2. Amphitheaters—Rome—Juvenile literature. 3. Rome (Italy)—Buildings, structures, etc.—Juvenile literature. 4. Rome (Italy)—Antiquities—Pictorial works—Juvenile
literature. [1. Colosseum (Rome, Italy)—Design and construction.
2. Rome (Italy)—Buildings, structures, etc. 3. Rome (Italy)—
Antiquities.]   I. Title.   II. Series.
DG68.1.N37   1998
725'.827'09376—dc21   97-2839
                                                                CIP
                                                                 AC

CONTENTS

FOREWORD

Throughout history, as civilizations have evolved and prospered, each has produced unique buildings and architectural styles. Combining the need for both utility and artistic expression, a society's buildings, particularly its large-scale public structures, often reflect the individual character traits that distinguish it from other societies. In a very real sense, then, buildings express a society's values and unique characteristics in tangible form. As scholar Anita Abromovitz comments in her book *People and Spaces*, "Our ways of living and thinking—our habits, needs, fear of enemies, aspirations, materialistic concerns, and religious beliefs—have influenced the kinds of spaces that we build and that later surround and include us."

That specific types and styles of structures constitute an outward expression of the spirit of an individual people or era can be seen in the diverse ways that various societies have built palaces, fortresses, tombs, churches, government buildings, sports arenas, public works, and other such monuments. The ancient Greeks, for instance, were a supremely rational people who originated Western philosophy and science, including the atomic theory and the realization that the earth is a sphere. Their public buildings, epitomized by Athens's magnificent Parthenon temple, were equally rational, emphasizing order, harmony, reason, and above all, restraint.

By contrast, the Romans, who conquered and absorbed the Greek lands, were a highly practical people preoccupied with acquiring and wielding power over others. The Romans greatly admired and readily copied elements of Greek architecture, but modified and adapted them to their own needs. "Roman genius was called into action by the enormous practical needs of a world empire," wrote historian Edith Hamilton. "Rome met them magnificently. Buildings tremendous, indomitable, amphitheaters where eighty thousand could watch a spectacle, baths where three thousand could bathe at the same time."

In medieval Europe, God heavily influenced and motivated the people, and religion permeated all aspects of society, molding people's worldviews and guiding their everyday actions. That spiritual mindset is reflected in the most important medieval structure—the Gothic cathedral—which, in a sense, was a model of heavenly cities. As scholar Anne Fremantle so elegantly phrases it, the cathedrals were "harmonious elevations of stone and glass reaching up to heaven to seek and receive the light [of God]."

Our more secular modern age, in contrast, is driven by the realities of a global economy, advanced technology, and mass communications. Responding to the needs of international trade and the growth of cities housing millions of people, today's builders construct engineering marvels, among them towering skyscrapers of steel and glass, mammoth marine canals, and huge and elaborate rapid transit systems, all of which would have left their ancestors, even the Romans, awestruck.

In examining some of humanity's greatest edifices, Lucent Books' Building History Series recognizes this close relationship between a society's historical character and its buildings. Each volume in the series begins with a historical sketch of the people who erected the edifice, exploring their major achievements as well as the beliefs, customs, and societal needs that dictated the variety, functions, and styles of their buildings. A detailed explanation of how the selected structure was conceived, designed, and built, to the extent that this information is known, makes up the majority of the volume.

Each volume in the Lucent Building History Series also includes several special features that are useful tools for additional research. A chronology of important dates gives students an overview, at a glance, of the evolution and use of the structure described. Sidebars create a broader context by adding further details on some of the architects, engineers, and construction tools, materials, and methods that made each structure a reality, as well as the social, political, and/or religious leaders and movements that inspired its creation. Useful maps help the reader locate the nations, cities, streets, and individual structures mentioned in the text; and numerous diagrams and pictures illustrate tools and devices that bring to life various stages of construction. Finally, each volume contains two bibliographies, one for student research, the other listing works the author consulted in compiling the book.

Taken as a whole, these volumes, covering diverse ancient and modern structures, constitute not only a valuable research tool, but also a tribute to the human spirit, a fascinating exploration of the dreams, skills, ingenuity, and dogged determination of the great peoples who shaped history.

IMPORTANT DATES IN THE BUILDING OF THE ROMAN COLOSSEUM

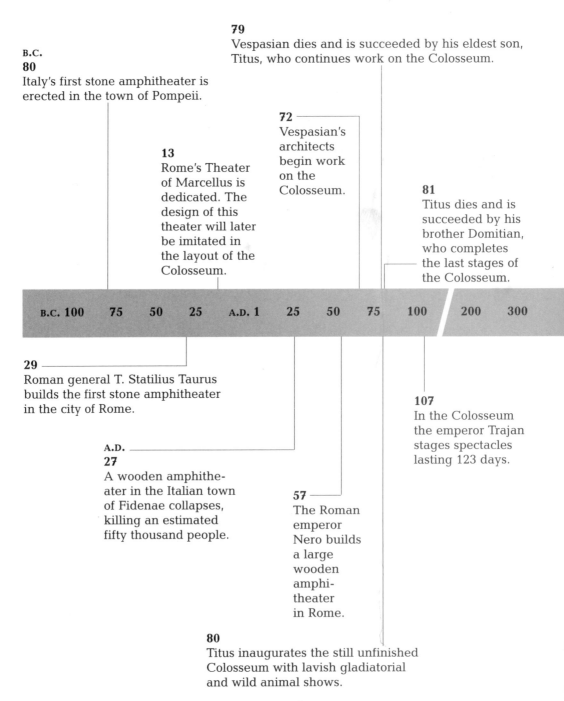

79
Vespasian dies and is succeeded by his eldest son, Titus, who continues work on the Colosseum.

B.C.
80
Italy's first stone amphitheater is erected in the town of Pompeii.

72
Vespasian's architects begin work on the Colosseum.

13
Rome's Theater of Marcellus is dedicated. The design of this theater will later be imitated in the layout of the Colosseum.

81
Titus dies and is succeeded by his brother Domitian, who completes the last stages of the Colosseum.

B.C. 100   75   50   25   A.D. 1   25   50   75   100   200   300

29
Roman general T. Statilius Taurus builds the first stone amphitheater in the city of Rome.

A.D.
27
A wooden amphitheater in the Italian town of Fidenae collapses, killing an estimated fifty thousand people.

107
In the Colosseum the emperor Trajan stages spectacles lasting 123 days.

57
The Roman emperor Nero builds a large wooden amphitheater in Rome.

80
Titus inaugurates the still unfinished Colosseum with lavish gladiatorial and wild animal shows.

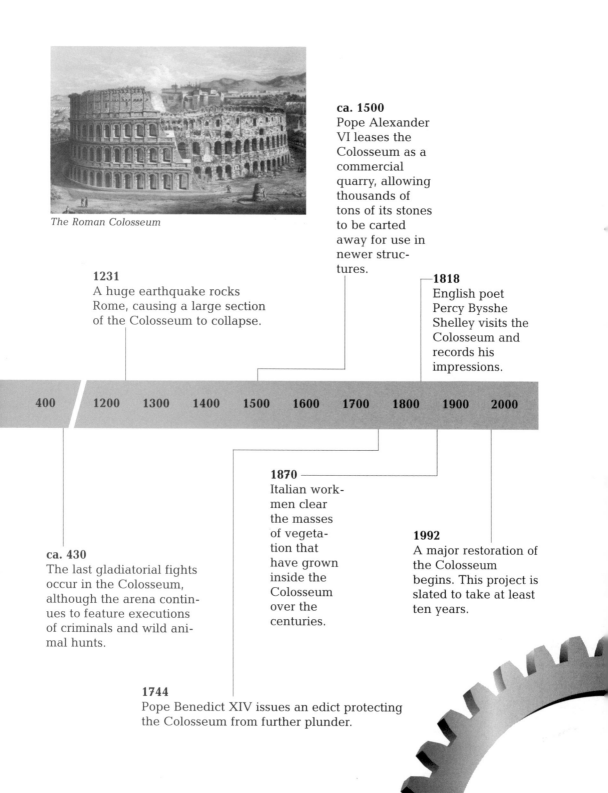

The Roman Colosseum

ca. 1500
Pope Alexander VI leases the Colosseum as a commercial quarry, allowing thousands of tons of its stones to be carted away for use in newer structures.

1231
A huge earthquake rocks Rome, causing a large section of the Colosseum to collapse.

1818
English poet Percy Bysshe Shelley visits the Colosseum and records his impressions.

400 1200 1300 1400 1500 1600 1700 1800 1900 2000

1870
Italian workmen clear the masses of vegetation that have grown inside the Colosseum over the centuries.

1992
A major restoration of the Colosseum begins. This project is slated to take at least ten years.

ca. 430
The last gladiatorial fights occur in the Colosseum, although the arena continues to feature executions of criminals and wild animal hunts.

1744
Pope Benedict XIV issues an edict protecting the Colosseum from further plunder.

Introduction

Bede, the medieval English theologian and historian, who later came to be known as the Venerable Bede, likely dreamed of visiting Rome. He knew that the famous "eternal city" had once been the capital of a mighty empire that, until its fall in the mid-fifth century A.D., had ruled the known world for some six centuries. But Bede never made the then long, arduous, and dangerous trip to Rome; and so he had to be content with the detailed descriptions of travelers who *had* completed the journey. Of all the Roman wonders they described, the most spectacular was a massive oval stone arena, a structure so gigantic that it had earned the nickname of Colosseum, a form of the Latin word *colosseus*, meaning "colossal." Believing that this great building, like the city of Rome itself, was an eternal symbol of the finest that humans had ever achieved, or would ever again achieve, Bede penned the now famous words:

> While stands the Colosseum, Rome shall stand,
> When falls the Colosseum, Rome shall fall,
> And when Rome falls—the world.

In the thirteen centuries since this epigram appeared, the Colosseum has remained the preeminent visual and romantic symbol of Rome's former greatness. And throughout most of those centuries, the building continued to dwarf all similar arenas. It was not until the construction of modern Olympic stadiums, like the one built in Greece in 1896, and football stadiums, such as the Yale Bowl erected in 1914 in Connecticut, that human beings produced public arenas with seating capacities greater than that of the Colosseum.

That a huge and magnificent building became Rome's lasting symbol was entirely appropriate, for the Romans were great builders, overall the most prolific, efficient, and practical in the ancient world. Indeed, as the noted scholar Edith Hamilton points out, the true Roman artist was not the painter, sculptor, or poet, but the engineer. "Roman genius was called into action by the enormous practical needs of a world empire," she wrote in her now classic book, *The Roman Way*. And Rome met these needs appropriately and magnificently by producing a vast network of roads for the swift transport of armies and trade goods; miles of aqueducts that supplied life-giving water to sustain thousands of cities and towns; as well as racetracks called "circuses," stadiums known as "amphitheaters," and public baths, which helped maintain order by keeping the Roman masses busy and entertained.

The Romans, however, did not invent roads, aqueducts, public baths, and sports stadiums. In fact, for the most part the Romans borrowed most of their cultural ideas from other lands. Describing this practice of his immediate ancestors, Sallust, the first-century B.C. Roman politician and historian, remarked, "Whatever they found suitable among allies or foes, they put in practice at home with the greatest enthusiasm, preferring to imitate rather than envy the successful." In the realm of architecture and building, for instance, the Romans adopted temple design mainly from the Greeks; and the structural concept of the arch, which became a Roman trademark, originated with the Etruscans, the inventive Italian people who had ruled Rome when it was still a crude farming community.

A view of Rome with the Colosseum in the background. The Romans borrowed their architectural styles from other societies, including the Greeks and the Etruscans.

Yet the Romans were no mere copiers. They possessed an amazing talent for combining foreign architectural ideas with their own native concepts and skills to produce structures special to their own practical needs. And even those constructions that the Romans adopted with little or no change reached grand heights of achievement in size, efficiency, durability, and sheer numbers that far surpassed any known before. The result was several types of structures, some old and some new, all of which came to be seen as uniquely Roman in character and application. Among these, as Edith Hamilton so movingly puts it, were

> buildings tremendous, indomitable, amphitheaters where eighty thousand could watch a spectacle, baths where three thousand could bathe at the same time, which nearly two thousand years have left practically intact. Bridges and aqueducts that spanned wide rivers and traversed great spaces with a beautiful, sure precision of soaring arches and massive piers. And always along with them the mighty Roman road, a monument of dogged, unconquerable human effort, huge stone jointed to huge stone, marching on and on irresistibly, through unknown hostile forests, over ramparts of mountains, across sun-baked deserts, to the very edges of the habitable world. That is the true art of Rome.

Out of this remarkable artistic tradition of grand-scale engineering and construction emerged what was probably the most popular Roman building of its own time and undeniably the most famous of later ages—the Colosseum. The stadium's original name was the Amphitheatrum Flavium, or Amphitheater of the Flavians. This referred to the fact that the emperor Vespasian, who began its construction, and his sons Titus and Domitian, who completed it, were members of the noble Flavian family line. Not until the Venerable Bede's time, long after the Roman Empire had fallen, did the name Colosseum come into general use.

Those medieval travelers who visited the empty and quiet—but still imposing—Colosseum had only vague notions about its actual use. As devout Christians, they had inherited the tradition of belief that in this arena Christian martyrs had

Roman workers lower a stone into place during the construction of a road near an aqueduct. The arches and piers of this aqueduct were similar to those used in the Colosseum.

once been thrown to hungry lions before crowds of "cruel and crazed" Roman pagans. And, indeed, it is possible that some early Christians had met grisly fates within the confines of the Colosseum's towering stone oval. However, the building's uses were much more varied and its history much more colorful and splendid than anything Bede and his medieval fellows could then imagine. The nature of the spectacles presented in what the nineteenth-century English poet Lord Byron called "a noble wreck in ruinous perfection," as well as the fascinating details of its construction, remained mysteries to be revealed by the pens and spades of later historians and archaeologists.

From Impermanent Wood to Durable Stone: Rome's First Amphitheaters

Although the Colosseum was the most spectacular and famous example of a Roman amphitheater, it was by no means the first such stadium erected in a Roman city. Long before its construction in the 70s and early 80s A.D., the need arose for arenas in which to stage gladiator fights, animal shows, and various other public games and spectacles. The first permanent Roman amphitheaters were built in the first century B.C., a tumultuous period in which one great Roman era, the Republic, was ending and another, the Empire, was beginning.

The Roman Republic and Roman Empire were two of the three general eras into which modern historians divide the approximately twelve centuries of Roman civilization. The first period, the "Kingship," in which kings ruled Rome, lasted from the city's traditional founding date in the 750s B.C. to 509 B.C. In that year, the richest and most powerful landowners threw out their king and established the Republic, which had a legislature known as the Senate and elected administrator-generals called consuls.

Rome then expanded outward from central Italy and by the beginning of the first century B.C. had carved out a huge realm consisting of all the lands bordering the Mediterranean Sea. During that fateful century, rocked by several devastating civil wars, the Republic fell and gave way to the Empire. In 27 B.C., Octavian, undisputed victor of the final civil war, took the name of Augustus, the "great and exalted one," and ruled as an absolute dictator; yet in his long reign, later called the Augustan Age, he proved himself a highly benevolent, constructive, and fair leader, even allowing the

Senate and consuls to remain (although he had the power to override them).

Most of Augustus's successors in the long line of Roman emperors who followed him, up until the Empire itself fell in A.D. 476, were not nearly as equitable and productive as he had been. However, several gained reputations as great builders, including the Flavians—Vespasian, Titus, and Domitian—who created the Colosseum. And among the many grand works of the important builder-emperors were other new amphitheaters to meet the growing demand for public arenas that had begun during the last years of the Republic.

EARLY WOODEN ARENAS

This increased public demand reflected a marked change in traditional Roman attitudes and values. Historians have determined that before the last two centuries of the Republic, the Romans were a largely conservative, austere people who considered most kinds of public displays, including shows and games, undignified. Although this rigid attitude softened appreciably in late republican times, it did so only slowly. Initially, public games and shows were not staged often enough to warrant the great expense of constructing large, permanent stone stadiums. The first public

Augustus, who became emperor in 27 B.C., was a fair and productive ruler.

shows took place in the forums, or main squares, of cities. We know this because of a reference made by the Augustan architect and engineer Vitruvius in his famous work, *De architectura*, or *On Architecture*: "The custom of giving gladiatorial shows in the forum has been handed down from our ancestors."

Eventually the Romans began building wooden arenas to accommodate public shows. It is likely that the first such structures consisted mainly of consecutive rows of seats set up in or around the forums where the games took place; however, in time these makeshift stadiums became separate, freestanding buildings in their own right. Some were dismantled and reassembled as need dictated. Others may have stood intact for several seasons before being demolished to make way for houses, temples, or other structures.

Though impermanent, these early arenas were often very large and elaborate, featuring seating for thousands or even tens of thousands of people. To build a typical stadium of this type required huge amounts of wood and nails and the labor of hundreds of builders and other craftsmen. This made the construction of such a stadium, like the often splendid games presented within it, an extremely expensive proposition that only wealthy aristocrats and businessmen could afford. Yet erecting stone amphitheaters was considerably *more* time-consuming and expensive; so even after the first stone versions appeared, people continued to supplement them with wooden ones.

Luckily, most of the individuals who financed wooden stadiums were responsible enough to hire skilled architects to ensure proper design and construction. But now and then, less reputable speculators trying to turn a fast profit hastily threw up amphitheaters that were poorly designed or built with substandard materials. Such shady practices occasionally led to disaster. In his *Annals*, the first-century A.D. historian Tacitus

Citizens are entertained by music and acrobatics in the Roman Forum. Rome's first public shows took place in the main squares of cities.

recorded the following gripping account of the collapse of a wooden arena in Fidenae, a town just north of Rome, in A.D. 27:

> An ex-slave called Atilius started building an amphitheater at Fidenae for a gladiatorial show. But he neither rested its foundations on solid ground nor fastened the wooden superstructure securely. He had undertaken the project not because of great wealth or municipal ambition but for sordid profits. Lovers of such displays . . . flocked in—men and women of all ages. Their numbers, swollen by the town's proximity, intensified the tragedy. The packed structure collapsed, subsiding both inwards and outwards and . . . overwhelming a huge crowd of spectators and bystanders. Those killed at the outset of the catastrophe at least escaped torture. . . . More pitiable were those, mangled but not yet dead, who knew their wives and children lay there too. In daytime they could see them, and at night they heard their screams and moans. . . . When the ruins began to be cleared, people rushed to embrace and kiss the corpses—and even quarreled over them, when features were unrecognizable but similarities of physique and age had caused wrong identifications. Fifty thousand people were mutilated or crushed in the disaster.

THE FIRST STONE AMPHITHEATERS

Stone amphitheaters were much sturdier, safer, and of course, more durable and permanent. The first stone stadium was erected about the year 80 B.C. in the small city of Pompeii, located on what is now the Bay of Naples, about 140 miles southeast of Rome. Because the now famous A.D. 79 volcanic eruption of nearby Mount Vesuvius encased the town in a protective layer of ash, the amphitheater is well preserved. In fact, the inscription carved to dedicate the building still survives, bearing the names of the two prominent public officials who constructed it—Valgus and Porcius. Because the Latin term *amphitheatrum* had not yet been coined, the inscription refers to the structure as a *spectacula*, or a "place for spectacles."

Also still plainly visible are the design details of the oval stadium, which measures 445 by 341 feet and originally seated

AMPHITHEATERS ACROSS THE EMPIRE

In the three centuries or so following the creation of the Pompeiian amphitheater, the first constructed entirely of stone masonry, the Romans built dozens of similar arenas throughout Italy and across the Empire. In addition to the largest and most famous—the Colosseum in Rome—these included the huge amphitheater at Capua, about 110 miles southeast of the capital, which measured 560 by 460 feet and stood 95 feet high; the arena at Puteoli (modern Pozzuoli), across the Bay of Naples from Pompeii, measuring 490 by 370 feet; northern Italy's impressive Verona amphitheater, with dimensions of 500 by 405 feet and a seating capacity of 25,000–28,000; and similarly large versions at Nîmes and Arles, both in Gaul, what is now France, and at Thysdrus, in northern Africa. Many towns had smaller, but no less beautiful and sturdy, arenas. Typical was the amphitheater at Trier, originally called Augusta Treverorum, a prosperous town on the Moselle River in northeastern Gaul. The masonry structure went up sometime in the early second century A.D., probably on the site where wooden versions had stood for some time. The amphitheater's bowl was about 230 feet long and accommodated approximately 7,000 people. The vast majority of such structures were built from scratch as oval shaped masonry shells with dirt arenas, also oval shaped, in their centers. However, a few—such as the arenas at Dodona, in western Greece, and Xanthos, in Asia Minor, what is now Turkey—had been Greek theaters, which had presented plays before the Romans converted them to accommodate gladiator fights and wild-beast shows.

some twenty thousand people, Pompeii's entire population. The arena floor, where the shows took place, is sunken below the level of the outside ground, so that an earthen embankment helps support the weight of many of the rising tiers of stone seats. Providing support for the stadium's curved walls are an outer perimeter of high brick arches and several large exterior staircases.

Despite their excellent state of preservation, the Pompeiian amphitheater's bare stones offer only a fragmentary impression of what the building was like in its glory. No longer visible are the many comforts and amenities the crowds of spectators enjoyed. Among these were elegant decorations such as statues and tapestries; cushions to sit on; fast-food stands surrounding the complex, as well as roving vendors selling refreshments in the stands; and a huge awning, or *velarium*, that shaded the audience on hot sunny days. That the awning above could be nearly as important to a spectator's enjoyment as the shows staged below is evidenced by an advertisement, which Vesuvius's ash preserved on a city wall: "The gladiatorial troop hired by Aulus Suettius Certus will fight in Pompeii on May 31. There will also be a wild animal hunt. The awnings will be used."

As for the shows themselves, apparently the violence staged in such stadiums occasionally spilled over into the audience. Tacitus told of a serious riot that occurred in Pompeii's arena in A.D. 59:

> There was a serious fight between the inhabitants of two [neighboring] Roman settlements, Nuceria and Pompeii. It arose out of a trifling incident at a gladiatorial show given by Livineius Regulus. . . . During an exchange of taunts—characteristic of these disorderly country towns—abuse led to stone-throwing, and then swords were drawn. The people of Pompeii, where the show was held, came off best. Many wounded and mutilated Nucerians were taken to the capital [Rome]. . . . The emperor [Nero] instructed the Senate to investigate the affair. The Senate passed it to the consuls. When they reported back, the Senate debarred Pompeii from holding any similar gathering for ten years. Illegal associations in the town were dissolved; and the sponsor of the show and his fellow-instigators of the disorders were exiled.

Because of the great expense of building and maintaining stone stadiums, for a long time few towns attempted to match Pompeii's achievement. Even in Rome, the capital of what was then the most powerful and prosperous empire in world history, building a properly grand stone amphitheater remained an elusive goal. In 29 B.C., fully half a century after the dedica-

tion of the Pompeiian arena, T. Statilius Taurus, one of Octavian's generals, constructed an amphitheater in Rome's Campus Martius, or Field of Mars, a large open area near the Tiber River. Because this arena no longer exists, historians are uncertain about its seating capacity. But it was surely far too small to satisfy the needs of a city the size of Rome, which by this time had a population of nearly a million. Another drawback was that, to save expense, Taurus's builders utilized both wood and stone, leaving the building more prone to damage by fire, which in fact eventually destroyed it.

The amphitheater at Pompeii was the first Roman stone stadium. It was preserved under the ash from the eruption of Mount Vesuvius in A.D. 79.

STILL NO PROPER ARENA IN THE CAPITAL

During the roughly nine decades in which Taurus's stadium remained intact, the early emperors evidently felt that it, supplemented by the temporary wooden versions erected from time to time, was enough to serve the capital. Around the year A.D. 57, for example, the infamous Nero, Augustus's great-great-grandson and the fifth Roman emperor, built a wooden amphitheater. According to the second-century A.D. historian Suetonius, the arena rose in the Campus Martius and took "less than a year" to build. In the inaugural show, Nero forced "400 senators and 600 knights [members of the Equestrian order; essentially well-to-do businessmen], some of them rich and respectable, [to] do battle in the arena; and some had to fight wild beasts and perform various duties about the ring." When the seating capacities of this and Taurus's arena proved inadequate, various games and shows were held in the Circus Maximus, the large elliptical track designed for chariot and horse racing.

Meanwhile, rather than build a stone arena of size and splendor appropriate to the capital of the known world, the emperors chose to spend their money on other enterprises. Again,

Nero was the most prominent example. Yet ironically, his failure to give Rome a proper amphitheater inspired a series of events that eventually led to the erection of just such a structure. Many of his building projects, widely perceived as wasteful and having no public benefit, set a negative precedent that his successors tried to reverse by building the Colosseum, a highly useful public facility. In fact, the mighty arena would end up occupying the very site of Nero's most extravagant and notorious creation.

The immediate chain of events leading to the Colosseum's conception began in A.D. 64, when a terrible fire devastated about two-thirds of Rome. The blaze began in the wooden seats of the Circus Maximus, raged for nine days, and destroyed thousands of homes, temples, and public buildings, including Taurus's amphitheater. Of the fourteen local regions into which Augustus had earlier divided the city, three were totally wiped out and only four escaped damage. To his credit, Nero organized shelters for the homeless and launched ambitious rebuilding projects. (The old adage about his starting the fire and reciting poetry while watching the city burn is almost certainly false.) In the process, he realigned many formerly winding streets on an efficient grid pattern and introduced a strict new building code that greatly reduced the risk of fires.

However, Nero devoted a larger portion of the state treasury to building projects that benefited him alone. One immense area the great fire had cleared stretched from the Palatine hill, the traditional site of the imperial residences, across the low, relatively flat expanse between the Esquiline and Caelian hills. Comprising nearly 350 acres of prime real estate in the heart of the city, this tract had room for dozens of public buildings, including perhaps a new and properly spectacular amphitheater. But Nero, a conceited and self-indulgent individual, decided to transform the entire area into his own personal pleasure park and palace.

A Monument to Himself

Under the direction of the emperor's talented architect, Severus, and chief engineer, Celer, what became known as the Domus Aurea, or Golden House, began to rise from the rubble left by the great fire. To many Romans, the Golden House seemed not only an unnecessary waste of money at a time when so many were in need, but also extremely out of place. The grandiose project was essentially a wealthy country villa set in the middle of the world's most crowded urban center. The living quarters alone covered some nine hundred thousand square feet, about 450 times the floor space of an average modern house. "The entrance-hall," wrote Suetonius, "was large enough to contain a huge statue of himself [Nero], 120 feet high." Created by the sculptor, Zenodoros, and patterned after the famous Colossus of Rhodes, one of the seven wonders of the ancient world, the towering figure became known as the Colossus of Nero. Outside of this palatial residence stretched a vast parkland containing gardens, meadows, fishponds, game preserves, streams, waterfalls, and a pillar-lined, roofed walkway nearly a mile long. Suetonius gave these further details of the emperor's "monument to himself":

ROME ENGULFED BY FLAMES

In this excerpt from his *Annals*, the Roman historian Tacitus describes the great fire that ravaged Rome in A.D. 64:

Now started the most terrible and destructive fire which Rome had ever experienced. It began in the Circus [Maximus], where it adjoins the Palatine and Caelian hills. Breaking out in shops selling inflammable goods, and fanned by the wind, the conflagration instantly grew and swept the whole length of the Circus. There were no walled mansions or temples, or any other obstructions, which could arrest it. First, the fire swept violently over the level spaces. Then it climbed the hills. . . . Terrified, shrieking women, helpless old and young, people intent on their own safety, people unselfishly supporting invalids or waiting for them, fugitives and lingerers alike—all heightened the confusion. When people looked back, menacing flames sprang up before them or outflanked [moved around in back of] them. When they escaped to a neighboring quarter, the fire followed—even districts believed to be remote proved to be involved. Finally, with no idea where or what to flee, they crowded on to the country roads, or lay in the fields. Some who had lost every-

An enormous pool, like a sea, was surrounded by build-ings made to resemble cities, and by a landscape garden consisting of plowed fields, vineyards, pastures, and woodlands—where every variety of domestic and wild animal roamed about. Parts of the house were overlaid with gold [giving the place its name] and studded with precious stones and mother-of-pearl. All the dining-rooms had ceilings of . . . ivory, the panels of which could slide back and let a rain of flowers, or of perfume from hidden sprinklers, shower upon his guests. The main dining room was circular, and its roof revolved, day and night, in time with the sky. Sea water, or sulfur water, was always on tap in the baths. When the palace

thing . . . could have escaped, but preferred to die. So did others, who had failed to rescue their loved ones. Nobody dared fight the flames. Attempts to do so were prevented by menacing gangs [of looters]. . . . Nero . . . returned to the city when the fire was approaching the mansion he had built to link the Gardens of Maecenas to the Palatine. The flames could not be prevented from overwhelming the whole of the Palatine, includ-ing his palace. Nevertheless, for the relief of the home-less, fugitive masses he threw open the Field of Mars . . . and even his own Gardens. Nero also constructed emergency accommodation for the destitute multitude. . . . By the sixth day enormous demolitions had con-fronted the raging flames with bare ground and open sky, and the fire was finally stamped out at the foot of the Esquiline hill. But before panic had subsided, or hope revived, flames broke out again in the more open regions of the city. Here there were fewer casualties; but the destruction of temples and pleasure arcades was even worse. . . . Of Rome's fourteen districts only four remained intact. Three were leveled to the ground. The other seven were reduced to a few scorched and mangled ruins.

had been decorated throughout in this lavish style, Nero dedicated it, and condescended to remark, "Good, now I can at last begin to live like a human being!"

But no other human beings in Rome lived nearly as well as Nero, who became increasingly self-centered, wasteful, politically corrupt, and cruel as his reign progressed. As suspicion of

This painting depicts Nero's persecution of the early Christians, whom he officially blamed for starting the great fire.

THE NEW BUILDING CODE

One of the few positive legacies of Nero's corrupt reign was the admirable and effective building code he instituted in the wake of the disastrous fire that leveled much of the city, in the process clearing the space for his Golden House and ultimately the Colosseum. New streets had to be broad and laid out in a regular grid pattern, as compared to the narrow, winding alleyways that had comprised much of the older city. Newly built houses and shops were required to have porticoes, or roofed walkways, in front so that in an emergency firefighters could stand on their flat roofs to fight the flames. Furthermore, no structure was permitted to stand more than seventy feet, or about seven stories, high, increasing the chances that all residents might escape during a fire; each house or apartment building had to be constructed independently, so that it did not share a wall with its neighbor, to make it more difficult for a fire to spread; and all new buildings had to contain a certain proportion of fire-resistant stone, as well as far less timber than in older-style structures. In addition, special officials had the task of ensuring that fountains and other local water supplies were always working and well maintained, and all householders were required to keep buckets and other fire-fighting equipment readily available. As still happens today, some people ignored or got around these regulations. But the majority observed them, as evidenced by the fact that while Rome witnessed later fires, none were as large or destructive as that of A.D. 64.

and hatred for him grew, unfounded rumors spread that he had started the great fire in order to clear the space for his Golden House. And failed assassination plots abounded, resulting in Nero's torturing, executing, or exiling hundreds of people. But though these plots were unsuccessful, the emperor's decadent days were numbered and his magnificent palace and parklands marked for a new round of large-scale urban renewal. For it was to be on these grounds that Nero's successors, in a conscious effort to bury the memory of his reign, would construct the mighty Colosseum. Ironically, from the wreckage of the colossal and impermanent symbol of one Roman's monstrous vanity would rise the equally colossal and eternal symbol of all the Romans as a great people.

Symbol of the New Flavian Rome: The Colosseum's Construction Begins

One of Nero's favorite spots on the splendid and picturesque grounds of his fabulous Golden House was his *stagnum*, an artificial lake his workmen had created and surrounded with lush greenery and quaint buildings. What the corrupt young emperor with spindly legs and a potbelly could not have imagined at the time was that soon this lake would be gone. In its place would rise the magnificent amphitheater that later generations would call the Colosseum. In fact, this lake was but one of Nero's works that were about to be swept away. During an infamous reign in which he constantly wasted public money on his own pleasures, murdered his own wife and mother, and repeatedly terrorized senators and other highborn individuals, he had outraged most Romans and made enemies of many powerful men.

"At last," as Suetonius put it, in the early months of A.D. 68, "after nearly fourteen years of Nero's misrule, the earth rid herself of him." The Roman legions in Spain proclaimed their commanding general, Galba, as emperor and soon afterward the Senate in Rome accepted this decision and declared the thirty-one-year-old Nero an enemy of the people. Fearing torture and execution, Nero chose suicide. An egotist to the end, he shouted, "What an artist the world is losing!" and then, with the aid of his secretary, stabbed himself in the throat. According to Suetonius, "He died, with eyes glazed and bulging from their sockets, a sight which horrified everybody present." Some said it was a fitting end for a cruel and pitiless tyrant.

Yet, though practically no one was sorry that Nero was gone, his death brought on a crisis the likes of which Rome had not faced since the bloody civil wars in the final years of the Republic. Galba was old and feeble; and after becoming emperor he made the mistake of refusing to pay the imperial bodyguards the bonuses he had promised them. So they promptly murdered him. In the power struggle that ensued, two other powerful generals, Otho and Vitellius, declared themselves emperor, as did Vespasian, the distinguished general who had the backing of the armies in Rome's eastern provinces, including Egypt. Because four men in all had claimed the imperial office in little more than a year, A.D. 69 thereafter became known as "the year of the four emperors." Vitellius managed to defeat Otho. But then Vespasian's forces marched on Rome and crushed those of Vitellius, whom Vespasian's soldiers dragged into the main forum, murdered, and threw into the Tiber. The way was now clear for Vespasian's establishment of the Flavian dynasty, whose chief contribution to posterity would be the Colosseum.

Roman emperor Vespasian.

AN HONEST AND HARDWORKING NEW EMPEROR

Vespasian, whose full name was Titus Flavius Vespasianus, was a very different sort of ruler than Nero had been. Besides being a decadent and self-centered person, Nero was an aristocrat who traced his family line back through the Julio-Claudian dynasty to the highborn Augustus and Julius Caesar. By contrast, Vespasian came from an upper-middle-class family of soldiers and civil servants. As a tax collector in the Roman province of Asia, Sabinus, Vespasian's father, had earned a reputation as an honest and hardworking man, and Vespasian displayed these same qualities as a professional soldier and also as emperor. Vespasian immediately established good relations with the senators and other aristocrats. They saw that he was a tolerant, frugal, and efficient bureaucrat interested only in restoring good government to Rome; and they were impressed with his strict economic policies, which steadily replenished a state treasury that had been drained by Nero's excesses.

Indeed, the main theme of Vespasian's reign was the creation of a new Rome, one of which all Romans could be proud.

To symbolize this goal, the coins he struck bore the motto *Roma resurgens*, meaning "Rome reborn." Rebuilding Rome was a monumental task, for although some of Nero's reconstruction programs in the wake of the great fire had been impressive, many sections of the city remained rubble or supported squalid shantytowns. In addition, the fighting during the recent civil war had destroyed other areas and monuments, including the temple of Jupiter, the chief god of the state religion. This building rested atop the Capitol, the sacred summit of the Capitoline hill. Rising to the task, Vespasian became one of Rome's notable emperor-builders. Suetonius recalled:

> In Rome, which had been made unsightly by fires and collapsed buildings, Vespasian authorized anyone who pleased to take over the vacant sites, and build on them if the original owners failed to come forward. He personally inaugurated the restoration of the burned Capitol, by collecting the first basketfull of rubble and carrying it away on his shoulders. . . . He also started work on several new buildings: a temple of Peace near the Forum, [and] a temple to Claudius [the fourth emperor and Nero's predecessor] . . . on the Caelian hill . . . [a structure] almost completely destroyed by Nero.

Vespasian also undertook a task long overdue in Rome—the construction of a stone public amphitheater of a size and splendor befitting the capital of the known world. To be sure, his motives for creating the new Flavian Amphitheater were not entirely unselfish. From the beginning, the structure was designed not only as a symbol of Roman greatness, but also as a showcase for the nobility and generosity of the new Flavian dynasty. Vespasian fully intended that his sons, Titus and Domitian, should succeed him and hoped that they would plant the seeds for a long-lived and productive line of rulers.

Yet at least this arena would not be a monument to one man, as Nero's Golden House had been. Hundreds of thousands of Romans of all walks of life would benefit each year from using the new amphitheater. In fact, Vespasian did everything he could to make the Colosseum a statement against Nero, his unpopular reign, and his very memory. As a first step, the new emperor chose as a building site Nero's precious artificial lake on the grounds of the pretentious and much-hated

The Temple of Jupiter, on top of Capitoline hill, was destroyed by the fire that swept Rome. Vespasian restored the temple and other buildings, and began several new construction projects, including the Colosseum.

Golden House. The huge Colossus of Nero was allowed to remain. But Vespasian ordered the likeness of the statue to be transformed from that of Nero into that of the sun god Helios by adding a crown of projecting solar rays to the figure's head. Some scholars believe that the Colossus's close proximity to the amphitheater may, in the centuries that followed, have given rise to the arena's later name—the Colosseum.

A Traditional Design

Another way the Colosseum was a statement against the Neronian past was in the building style chosen by Vespasian and his imperial architect, whose identity remains unknown. Nero had been a flamboyant, showy person who enjoyed experimentation and daring new artistic styles, including novel architectural ideas. These reached their zenith in the design of the Golden House. Before the advent of this gaudy but brilliantly designed structure, the style of most Roman houses and palaces was fairly utilitarian and unimaginative, consisting of corridors with rows of doors leading to standard rectangular rooms having flat roofs. By contrast, the Golden House successfully utilized the concept of expanded interior space. It featured numerous rooms having domed roofs, which gave a feeling of tremendous interior space; and many of these chambers had few separating walls, so that they seemed to flow together into wide-open, shared spaces. Eventually this innovative and visually attractive style would become common in Roman building, especially in large public structures.

But Vespasian was as conservative and tradition-oriented as Nero was liberal and modernistic. Although the new emperor wanted a new Rome, he desired it to return to traditional values, ideas, and styles that, he believed, had helped make the Romans masters of the Mediterranean world. Specifically, Vespasian and his architects chose to emulate the architectural styles that predominated in the late Republic and early Empire, the era of the great conqueror Julius Caesar and of Augustus. The first Roman emperor, like the present one, had been a con-

VITRUVIUS: AN ARCHITECT FOR THE AGES

Little is known about the life of Marcus Vitruvius Pollio, beyond that he was a practicing Roman architect from about 46 to 30 B.C. This was the period encompassing the last two years of Julius Caesar's dictatorship and the ensuing civil war that brought down the Republic and resulted in Augustus's establishment of the Empire. Vitruvius was apparently already an old man by the late 20s B.C., when he penned the ten books comprising his great treatise— *De architectura*, or *On Architecture*. In the preface of the work, he explained that it was dedicated to his mentor, Augustus, saying:

> I set about the composition of this work for you. For I perceived that you have built, and are now building, on a large scale. Furthermore, with respect to the future, you have such regard to public and private buildings, that they will correspond to the grandeur of our history, and will be a memorial to future ages. . . . In the following books, I have expounded a complete system of architecture.

This last sentence was no idle boast; for the work covers all types of Greek and Roman building, as well as methods

servative, tradition-oriented ruler; and, indeed, Vespasian envisioned himself as a new Augustus reconnecting Rome to its time-honored, glorious past.

Not surprisingly then, Vespasian's architects used the book written by the conservative Augustan architect Vitruvius as an architectural bible. And it was no accident that the principal model for the Colosseum was one of the most famous public buildings erected by Augustus—the Theater of Marcellus. The theater was named after Augustus's beloved nephew, who had died prematurely a few years before its dedication in 13 B.C. According to varying modern estimates, it sat anywhere from eleven thousand to fifteen thousand spectators. Having the shape of a hemisphere, like half a pie, the building's curved wall enclosed rising tiers of seats, while its

of decoration, mathematics, and diverse aspects of civil engineering. Book One deals with the qualifications of an architect and with town planning; Book Two covers building materials, including brick and concrete; Book Three describes temple architecture; Book Four, the three decorative orders of columns; Book Five, public buildings and how sound propagates within them; Book Six, private dwellings; Book Seven, interior decorations; Book Eight, aqueducts and water systems; Book Nine, geometry, astronomy, and measuring; and Book Ten, mechanics and mechanical devices, including catapults and other war machines.

Vitruvius's prediction about his conservative "Augustan" style becoming a memorial for future ages turned out to be correct. After Rome's fall, *De architectura* survived in various medieval handwritten copies. The edition published in 1486 became a sudden sensation among European architects and established the neoclassical building style that dominated Europe for centuries to come and even influenced American architects such as Thomas Jefferson.

Vitruvius, first-century B.C. Roman architect.

straight wall, elegantly decorated on the side facing the audience, provided a backdrop for the semicircular stage.

To support the theater's heavy stone superstructure and seating, the builders employed two of the three most important basic hallmarks of Roman construction—the arch and the vault. A typical Roman arch began with two vertical supports, called piers. Curving inward from the top of each pier was an arc of wedge-shaped stones, known as voussoirs (pronounced voo-SWARS), which met the other arc at the central keystone at the top. A Roman vault was a three-dimensional version of an arch—in effect, a curved ceiling. The Theater of Marcellus featured elegant-looking arcades, or rows of arches, on the outside wall, each of which opened into a barrel vault, a corridor with a curved ceiling running along its length. Commenting on the building's structure, the noted architectural historian J. B. Ward-Perkins explains how some of its barrel-vaulted corridors

> were radially disposed [fanning outward from the center like wheel spokes], incorporating an ingeniously contrived system of ascending ramps and annular [ring-like] corridors [intersecting the radial corridors like in-

Augustus's Theater of Marcellus was a model for the Colosseum. The theater's rising tiers of seats, radial barrel vaults, and arcades were used in the Flavian Amphitheater.

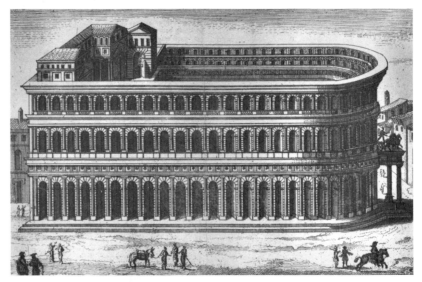

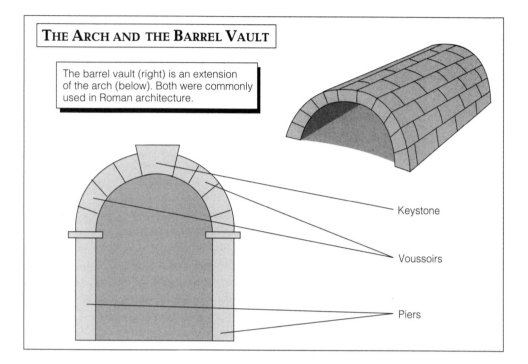

THE ARCH AND THE BARREL VAULT

The barrel vault (right) is an extension of the arch (below). Both were commonly used in Roman architecture.

Keystone

Voussoirs

Piers

ner and outer wheel rims] for the [entrances and exits] of the spectators . . . who sat in three ascending tiers of seats, each tier pitched more steeply than the one be-low it. . . . The outer corridor was vaulted with a series of radially disposed barrel vaults carried on massive . . . architraves [horizontal beams of stone or timber], one bay to each compartment of the façade [outer shell], in order to counteract the outward thrust of the upper tiers of seating.

The plans for the new Flavian Amphitheater called for us-ing these same architectural elements—arcades of arches, and barrel vaults set in a radial pattern to support rising tiers of seats. The main difference was that the newer structure would carry these elements around the full perimeter of an ellipse, or oval—essentially a slightly elongated circle—so that the the-ater's hemisphere would be doubled to form a full sphere in the amphitheater. This basic idea was certainly not new, for all stone amphitheaters since the first, in Pompeii, had employed it. In fact, the Latin word *amphitheatrum* translates literally as "double theater." What made the planned Flavian arena

PROPER RAMPS AND EXITS

While discussing formal theaters in his *De architectura*, Vitruvius offered the following advice about the construction of seating, gangways (curved ramps running in front of seating sections), passages (barrel-vaulted corridors connecting a structure's exterior and interior), and exits. Since Roman architects looked upon an amphitheater as, in essence, a double theater, Vespasian's architects followed most of this advice in their design for the Flavian Amphitheater.

> Above the foundations, the stepped seats ought to be built up from the substructure in stone or marble. The curved level gangways, it seems, should be made proportionally to the height of the theater; and each of them not higher at the back, than is the breadth of the passage of the gangway. . . . In brief the [typical] section of the theater is to be managed that if a line is drawn touching the lowest and the top rows, it shall also touch the front angles of all the rows. . . . Many spacious and stepped passages must be arranged between the seats; but the upper ones ought to be discontinuous [alternating] with the lower. Everywhere, each passage (upper or lower) must be continuous and straight without bends; so that when the audience is dismissed from the spectacle, it may not be cramped, but may find everywhere separate and uninterrupted exits.

A cutaway view of the right side of the Colosseum reveals the gangways circling the arena. Each of the arched passages on the bottom level, seen on the left side of the diagram, was an exit.

unique was its tremendous size—specifically a seating capacity twice as large as in any amphitheater yet built.

LAYING THE FOUNDATION

The first step in the Colosseum's construction, which began in A.D. 72, was to drain Nero's *stagnum*. This done, the next steps were to prepare the ground and lay in the foundation, which had to be perfectly level in order properly to support the massive vertical superstructure that would rise above it. Roman surveyors, called *agrimensores* (often *mensors* for short; another term for surveyor was *librator*), used a leveling device called a *chorobates*. According to Vitruvius, this was

> a straight plank about twenty feet long. At the extreme ends it has legs made to correspond [with each other], and fastened at right angles to the ends of the plank, and, between the plank and the legs, cross-pieces joined by tenons [wooden joints]. These have lines accurately drawn to a perpendicular [vertical line at a right angle to the horizontal], and plummets [plumb bobs, or small metal weights] hanging . . . over the lines from the plank. When the plank is in position, the perpendiculars which touch equally and of like measure the lines marked, indicate the level position of the instrument.

Once one side of the *chorobates* was in place, the surveyor kept slipping chocks, wooden wedges, under the other end until the plumb lines matched up with vertical lines drawn on the crosspieces. To double-check a reading's accuracy, he could pour water into a narrow *canalis*, or channel, in the top of the instrument. "If the water evenly touches the lips of the channel," wrote Vitruvius, "we shall know that the leveling is successful." Then the surveyor looked through two eyeholes cut into the plank and "sighted" the distant terrain or foundation to observe how much it would need to be leveled in order to line up with the instrument's reading.

The foundation had to be tremendously strong as well as level, for millions of tons of stone, wood, people, and animals would eventually press down on it. Unlike the partly sunken Pompeiian amphitheater, which rested much of its weight on solid earth, the Flavian arena was to be freestanding and aboveground. This meant that all of the building's weight would have to be supported by the walls, piers, and arches that rested on the artificial foundation. An added complication was that the Colosseum's design, also unlike that of the Pompeiian version, called for a maze of underground cellars, chambers, and corridors, so that great care would have to be taken to ensure that the weight of the upper stories did not fall over these empty spaces. Vitruvius gave this warning about solid supports:

> Buildings which start from the level of the ground, if the foundations are so laid . . . will assuredly be solid and durable. But if there are spaces underground and vaulted cellars, the foundations must be wider than the structures in the upper parts of the building. The party walls, the piers, the columns, are to be placed with their centers perpendicularly above the lower parts, so as to correspond to the solid [sections of the foundation]. For if the weight of the dividing walls or of the columns is over open spaces, it cannot be permanently sustained.

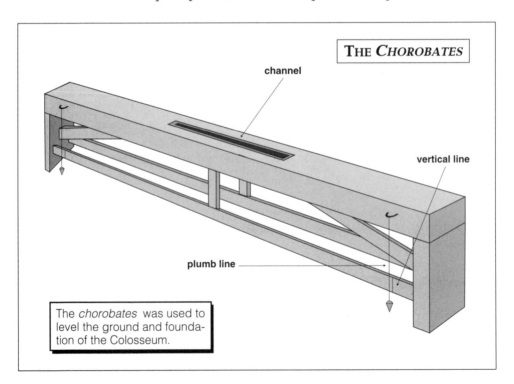

THE *CHOROBATES*

channel

vertical line

plumb line

The *chorobates* was used to level the ground and foundation of the Colosseum.

The underground chambers of the Colosseum, once covered by the arena floor, are visible in the lower right corner of this photo.

The material making up the Colosseum's foundation constituted the third of the three basic and characteristic elements of
Roman construction—concrete. Sometime in the third century
B.C., Roman builders discovered that adding a special kind of
sand to lime, in a ratio of two or three to one, produced a ce-
ment of rocklike hardness and great strength. Found near
Mount Vesuvius and other volcanoes, this sand was actually
volcanic ash laid down in prehistoric eruptions. Because the
main source of the material was Puteoli, on Vesuvius's slopes,
the mortar it produced came to be called *pulvis Puteolanus*.
The modern term "mortar" itself derives from *mortarium*, the
wooden trough in which Roman masons mixed the volcanic
sand and lime with water.

These masons made concrete by mixing wet *pulvis Puteolanus* with coarse sand and gravel. The usual method was to lay down a layer of wet mortar, press in a layer of gravel, lay down more mortar, add another level of gravel, and so on until they had achieved the desired thickness. In the case of the Colosseum's foundation, this was very thick indeed. In a huge hole excavated on the site of Nero's lake, workers created a monumental slab of concrete measuring 40 feet deep by 170 feet wide. This was intended to support the massive *cavea*, or central stone seating complex. Spreading outward from the upper half of this inner foundation was a 20-foot-thick concrete ring to support the building's outer shell of walls and piers.

ERECTING THE SUPERSTRUCTURE

These walls and piers, along with the complex of arches and vaults they supported, formed the great amphitheater's skeleton, or superstructure. The skeleton's vertical elements had to be as perfectly perpendicular as the horizontal foundation was perfectly level. To ensure exact right angles at all times, the workmen used an instrument called a *groma*. In his well-known book *The Ancient Engineers*, historian L. Sprague de Camp explains: "This was a pair of boards fastened together to make a right-angled cross, mounted horizontally atop a post or stand. Plumb lines, hanging from the four ends of the crosspieces, made it possible to level the instrument, and the surveyor sighted along the crosspieces."

The building's first vertical layer was actually located underground, where it was intended to remain hidden from the spectators. This was the complex of chambers that honeycombed the space directly beneath the arena's floor. Among these chambers were temporary quarters for the gladiators and other performers; cages for the lions, bears, elephants, and other animals that appeared in the public shows; mechanical elevators to transport both humans and beasts to the arena floor; and vast storage facilities. This subterranean complex also featured several long entry and connecting corridors, called *cryptoportici*.

The piers and vaulting located directly beneath the arena floor, which was composed of timber covered with earth, had only a relatively minimal load to support; whereas the piers in

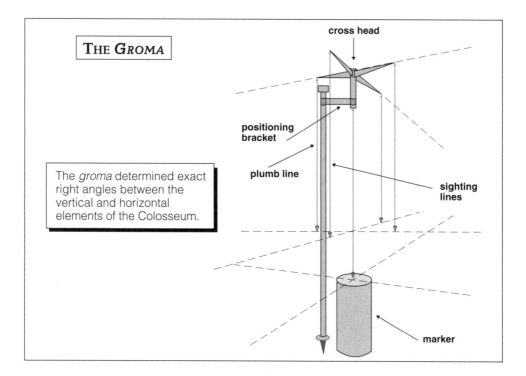

THE GROMA

cross head

positioning
bracket

plumb line

sighting
lines

marker

The *groma* determined exact
right angles between the
vertical and horizontal
elements of the Colosseum.

the building's first aboveground vertical layer had to bear the
huge weight of the stone *cavea* and outer superstructure. The
principal material used in these crucial load-bearing piers and
supports was travertine, a kind of limestone that was not only
tough and durable, but also attractive, having a fine, creamy-
white texture. The main source of travertine was the quarries
at Tibur (modern Tivoli), about twenty-five miles northeast of
Rome. The walls running between the travertine piers (both
radial and annular) were composed either of concrete faced
with bricks or of *tufa*, a stone formed of compressed volcanic
ash, faced with slabs of travertine. The workmen were divided into gangs, each of which specialized in one kind of
construction. Some gangs did nothing but erect travertine
piers, for instance, while others followed them around in-
stalling the *tufa* walls.

Meanwhile, other groups of workmen hauled the loads of
materials from Puteoli, Tibur, and dozens of other faraway
Italian sites. This was a gigantic and daunting task, for some
of the stones used in the structure were fifteen feet long, with
a volume of seventy cubic feet and a weight of five to six tons.

In all, the Colosseum encompassed over three and a half million cubic feet of stone! This and the other materials that went into the initial stages of the project required the constant use of an estimated two hundred wagons drawn by four hundred oxen. At any one moment, about a quarter of these wagons were loading at various supply sites, another quarter were unloading at the construction site, and the rest, some full and others empty, were traveling along the roads to or from Rome. In addition to the thousands of haulers, surveyors, masons, and other workmen, there were hundreds of toolmakers, blacksmiths, cart makers, bakers and other food suppliers, water bearers, rope makers, carpenters, sculptors, painters, and other supporting personnel. A staff of overseers, who took their orders directly from the architect, kept the immense ebb and flow of people and materials organized and running smoothly.

As this veritable army of craftsmen and laborers toiled away year after year, step by grueling step the amphitheater's superstructure rose above what had once been Nero's quiet pleasure grounds. Vespasian himself no doubt visited the busy construction site from time to time, for he was eager personally to present the new arena to the Roman people in opening ceremonies grander than any witnessed before. But the old soldier did not live to see his monument to Roman greatness completed and inaugurated. With his death in A.D. 79, that privilege passed to his equally eager sons, Titus and Domitian.

"The Tall Scaffolds Rise": The Colosseum Completed and Inaugurated

Though construction on the new Flavian Amphitheater had continued steadily for seven years, the huge project was still a long way from completion when Vespasian died. According to Suetonius, the emperor "caught a slight fever" but stubbornly carried on his duties even as his condition worsened. Finally, he became violently ill with chills and diarrhea. He "struggled to rise, muttering that an emperor ought to die on his feet, and collapsed in the arms of the attendants who went to his rescue. This was 23 June, A.D. 79, and he had lived sixty-nine years, seven months, and seven days."

With Vespasian's passing, his eldest son, Titus Flavius Vespasianus, inherited both the imperial titles and the task of finishing the Colosseum. Titus had many admirable qualities and talents. Suetonius recorded that

Titus (pictured) became emperor after his father Vespasian's death.

> he was both graceful and dignified, both muscular and handsome, except for a certain paunchiness. He had a phenomenal memory, and displayed a natural aptitude alike for almost all the arts of war and peace; handled arms and rode a horse with great skill; could compose speeches and verses in Greek and Latin with equal ease.

Like his father, Titus proved to be a remarkably fair, honest, and efficient ruler. One of the new emperor's first official acts, which won him the praise and respect of Romans of all classes, was to round up, severely flog, and then banish informers, people paid by one individual or group to spy on another individual or group. Titus also took a keen interest in his subjects. He would often have friendly conversations with the poorest and humblest of them at public games or in the bathhouses and happily listened to their grievances and did them favors. He was widely loved and the Roman people were genuinely saddened when he died unexpectedly (apparently of a fever), in September of A.D. 81, at the age of forty-one. Had he lived longer, Titus might have become one of Rome's greatest rulers; as it turned out, the most memorable legacy of his two-year reign was the lavish inaugural ceremony in which he opened the still unfinished Colosseum.

THE LOVE OF A FATHER FOR HIS CHILDREN

In addition to the splendid inaugural ceremonies for the Colosseum, Titus's short reign of twenty-six months and twenty days was marked by several other noteworthy events, including three large-scale natural catastrophes that struck within a few months of one another. The first disaster, which occurred on August 24, A.D. 79, just two months after Titus became emperor, was the great eruption of Mount Vesuvius in Campania, the region bordering the Bay of Naples. The historian Pliny the Younger, then a young man, happened to be staying nearby and later, in a letter to a friend, he penned a description that said in part:

> On the landward side a fearful black cloud was rent by forked and quivering bursts of flame, and parted to reveal great tongues of fire, like flashes of lightning magnified in size. . . . Many [people] besought the aid of the gods, but still more imagined that there were no gods left, and that the universe was plunged into eternal darkness evermore.

The eruption virtually destroyed the towns of Pompeii, Herculaneum, and Stabiae, leaving thousands of people homeless. Titus responded quickly and generously, showing, as Suetonius put it in *Lives of the Twelve Caesars,*

The Roman people disliked Titus's younger brother, Titus Flavius Domitianus, known simply as Domitian, as much as they had loved and respected the first two Flavians. Although he showed himself an able and efficient administrator, especially in the early years of his rule, over time Domitian revealed the cruel and twisted dimensions of his personality. Increasingly insecure and paranoid, he eventually initiated a reign of terror in which he murdered and exiled numerous senators and public officials and alienated the rest. Finally, many in high places, including his wife, Domitia, decided it would be best for Rome to get rid of him. Following a carefully orchestrated plot, on September 18, A.D. 96, a group of palace attendants attacked Domitian in his own quarters. "Stephanus

---

far more than an emperor's concern: it resembled the deep love of a father for his children, which he conveyed . . . by helping the victims to the utmost extent of his purse. He set up a board of ex-consuls . . . to relieve distress in Campania, and devoted the property of those who had died in the eruption and left no heirs to a fund for rebuilding the stricken cities.

Early in A.D. 80, while Titus was paying his second visit to the eruption victims in Campania, a terrible fire swept through Rome. The blaze destroyed many important buildings, including the Temple of Jupiter on the Capitoline hill, which had only recently been rebuilt after its destruction in the great fire of A.D. 64. Again demonstrating sincere concern and generosity, Titus stripped decorations from his own villas to replace those lost in some of the public buildings. About a year later, a plague (the identity of which remains unknown) struck Rome and still again Titus outdid himself attempting to provide aid. According to Suetonius, he resorted "to all sorts of sacrifices and medical remedies." It is no wonder that the Roman people expressed genuine sadness at this ruler's untimely death in September A.D. 81.

stabbed him in the groin," Suetonius wrote. "The wounded Domitian put up a fight but succumbed to seven further stabs." Besides his cruelties and assassination, posterity would remember Domitian most for completing the construction of the Colosseum, which would long outlive all of his successors and the empire they ruled.

CONSTRUCTION OF THE UPPER LEVELS

Under Vespasian, the imperial builders had installed the Flavian Amphitheater's massive concrete foundations and towering skeleton of travertine piers, arches, and vaults. During the last years of Vespasian's reign and the first of Titus's, the building's four major levels, or stories, rose above the hustle and bustle of the construction site. These stories were much larger than those of modern buildings, which tend to measure about nine to 11 feet each in height. The Colosseum's first level was over 34 feet high; the second, over 38 feet; the third, about 38 feet; and the fourth, over 45 feet. Thus, at over 156 feet, the combined height of the arena's four levels was approximately equivalent to that of a modern fifteen-story building.

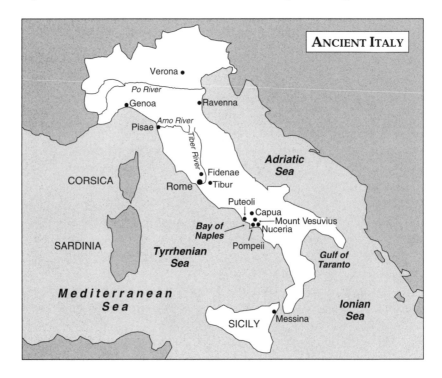

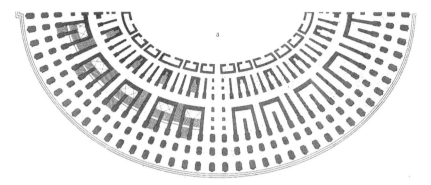

A half ground plan of the Colosseum reveals the radial passages crossing the curving corridors. The left side of the plan also shows the stairs to upper levels.

Each of the amphitheater's levels had varying numbers of seating rows in the *cavea*. And each seating section featured numerous exits leading into straight barrel-vaulted corridors that fanned away toward the building's outer perimeter. These radial passages intersected with the long, curving corridors, also in the shape of barrel vaults, that encircled the structure's outer sections. Each of the first three levels had eighty radial passages connecting the outermost corridor to the inner *cavea*.

Obviously, the mechanical engineering and manual labor needed to erect these levels were least daunting in the case of the first, since it was closest to the ground. As the workmen added each successive level, however, their tasks became increasingly difficult. To support themselves and their tools while working on the upper sections, they had to erect elaborate scaffolding, which must have temporarily encased the building in a wooden cocoon. The widely popular poet and humorist Martial, who enjoyed the patronage, or artistic support, of both Titus and Domitian, described how "in the middle way the tall scaffolds rise . . . where the far-seen Amphitheater lifts its august mass." Architectural historian Jean-Pierre Adam gives the following description of Roman scaffolding:

> In the case of both large construction and masonry, scaffolding remained a light structure, simply intended to support the workmen, their tools and small-size material; neither lifting machines nor heavy blocks could be placed on it. The wood used in its construction was therefore fairly small in section: poles, logs and planks.

A GREAT BUILDER-EMPEROR

Domitian's completion of the Colosseum was only one minor aspect of his ambitious building program, as explained in this excerpt from noted architectural historian J. B. Ward-Perkins's *Roman Imperial Architecture*.

His [Domitian's] work, viewed as a whole, may be regarded as broadly progressive . . . [and] by its very quantity [left] its mark upon Roman architecture at a critical stage in its development. It included, moreover, the creations of Rabirius, one of the few Roman architects of distinction whose name is known to us. Domitian has every right to be considered one of the great builder-emperors. Domitian's work may conveniently be discussed under three headings: buildings that he inherited unfinished from his father or his brother; those that he restored after the great fire of 80; and those that he initiated . . . although he did not in all cases live to complete them. To the first category belong the Colosseum, the Baths of Titus, and the Temple of Vespasian. . . . The fire of 80 left a heritage of buildings damaged or destroyed which . . . ranged

. . . Freestanding scaffolding had to support itself and of necessity rested on the ground. . . . The vertical supports were long pieces of wood simply stripped and retaining their natural shape, called standards. . . . At regular heights, depending on the requirements of the work, horizontal pieces joined two scaffolding poles to one another; the long longitudinal pieces (parallel to the wall) are the ledgers; the ones at right angles and supporting the boards, are the putlogs or putlocks. The whole thing is made stable by the diagonal pieces of bracing . . . and by sloping props resting on the ground.

To add extra support for unusually high buildings like the Colosseum, the workers "socketed" the scaffolding, or inserted the inner ends of the putlogs into small holes cut into the masonry. These holes, some of which were left in place as air

from the Temple of Jupiter . . . to the great complex of monuments built by Agrippa [Augustus's friend and adviser] in the *Campus Martius*. Almost without exception the buildings destroyed are known to have been restored by Domitian. . . . The Temple of Jupiter was once again restored on traditional lines, with a wealth of fittings such as gilded bronze tiles and doors plated with gold. . . . The buildings initiated by Domitian himself cover a remarkably wide range of techniques and architectural styles. At one end of the scale we have the Flavian Palace . . . Domitian's enduring monument . . . known officially as the Domus Augustana and in popular usage as the Palatium. . . . The architect was Rabirius. . . . It was an ingenious and on the whole very successful answer to the problem of combining the conflicting requirements of a palace and a private residence. . . . With remarkably few additions and modifications . . . Domitian's building was to remain the official Roman residence right down to late antiquity [ancient times], the . . . precursor of all subsequent "palaces."

vents or decorative touches, are still visible today in the ruins of many Roman buildings.

Because the workers could neither lift large stones to great heights using muscle power alone, nor rest such stones on the wooden scaffolding, they used various lifting devices, including large cranes. One of the most ingenious and powerful of these cranes utilized a circular cage, or drum, in which several workers operated a treadmill. Recommending the device for "loads of immense dimensions and weight," Vitruvius described it as having a tall wooden block, or support, surrounded by an elaborate system of ropes and pulleys. The ends of the ropes, he wrote,

> are carried back on the outside of the upper block and are taken over its lower pulleys, and return below. They are passed from the inside to the pulleys of the

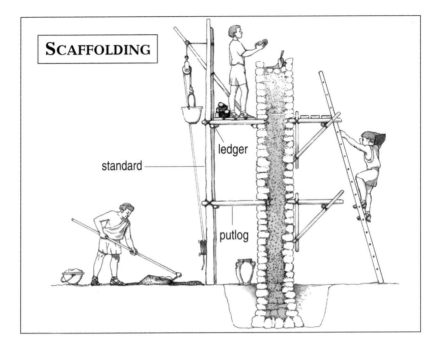

SCAFFOLDING

ledger

standard

putlog

lower block and are carried up right and left and return to the top round the highest pulleys. Passing from
the outside they are carried right and left of the drum
on the axle, and are tied so as to hold there. Then another rope is wound round the drum . . . and the drum,
being trodden by men, can produce [quick] results.

A sculpted relief of this very machine, with five men operating
the treadmill, was discovered in the tomb of the Haterii family,
a monument archaeologists have dated to the time of Domitian.
That his builders used the device to raise the stones of the
Colosseum's last and uppermost level is virtually certain.

THE OUTER FACADE

That uppermost level, the fourth, was the only one without
arches in its outer facade. The lower three levels had one large
arch for each of the eighty radial passageways leading outward
from (or inward toward) the *cavea*. Thus, the facade of each of
these levels constituted a gigantic and unbroken elliptical arcade of arches; and since each level had 80 arches, there were
240 arches in all. The 80 arches on the bottom level were entranceways, or *vomitoria*, measuring twenty-three feet high

and fourteen feet wide, through which spectators entered or exited the building. Each of the arches on the second and third levels was twenty-one feet high and fourteen feet wide.

For the most part, the outer facade was plain, befitting the conservatism of the structure's late republican architectural design. One exception was the addition of half-columns between and of the same height as the arches. Having no structural function, these columns were purely decorative. Each level displayed one of the three architectural orders that the Romans had borrowed from the Greeks—the Doric, with simple, flat column capitals, or tops; the Ionic, with capitals featuring volutes, or scrolls; and the most ornate, the Corinthian, with capitals covered with masonry leaves.

Roman architects did not utilize these orders randomly, as many modern builders do. Rather, each order had a symbolic meaning, depending on the kind of building in which it was used, and also produced a specific visual effect. Vitruvius devoted a great deal of space in his *De architectura* to the benefits and correct uses of the orders, saying, for example, the following about the Corinthian:

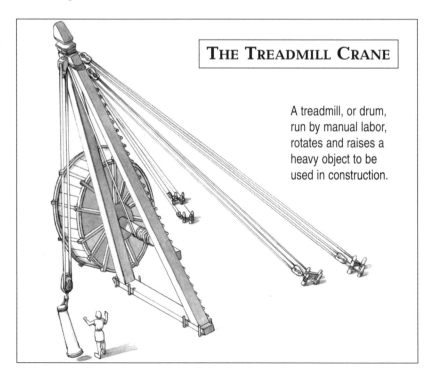

THE TREADMILL CRANE

A treadmill, or drum, run by manual labor, rotates and raises a heavy object to be used in construction.

Corinthian columns have all their proportions like the Ionic, with the exception of their capitals. The height of the capitals renders them proportionally higher and more slender, because the height of the Ionic capital is one-third of the thickness of the column, that of the Corinthian is the whole diameter of the shaft. Therefore because two-thirds of the diameter of the Corinthian columns are added to the capitals they give an appearance of greater slenderness owing to the increase in height.

For reasons that remain unknown, the Colosseum's architect chose to mix all three orders in the building's facade. The lowest level had half-columns of the Doric order, the second level, Ionic, and the third level, Corinthian. The archless fourth level featured forty-five-foot-high pilasters, or rectangular (rather than rounded) ornamental half-columns, having Corinthian capitals.

The other decorative feature of the amphitheater's outer facing consisted of a series of statues, one standing in each of the archways of the second and third levels. These figures, along with the columns, capitals, and other carving work, were cut and shaped with iron tools that included a cutting hammer (resembling an ax), a scabbling hammer (resembling a pick), a kivel (a tool having a head with a vertical edge on one side and a horizontal edge on the other), a punch (resembling a long railroad spike), and various mallets and chisels.

The Colosseum's exterior featured half-columns on each level. The bottom level's columns had plain Doric capitals (left), the second level had Ionic capitals (center), and the third level had ornate Corinthian capitals (right).

The chisels created the close detail work. With the driver chisel (driver, for short), for example, which had a cutting edge shaped in a right angle, a mason could carve perfect corners; and the gouge chisel (gouge, for short) had a concave cutting edge that produced curves and scoops of varying sizes and shapes for moldings.

DETAILS OF THE COMPLETED STRUCTURE

Once the outer facade and other decorative details had been added, the amphitheater was complete. In its original majesty, the building's oval bowl measured 620 by 513 feet in breadth and over 156 feet in height. The oval arena floor, outlined by and butting up against a protective wall at the bottom of the *cavea*, was 287 feet long by 180 feet wide.

Because the structure's seating sections no longer exist, the exact seating capacity is unknown, but most historians agree on an estimate of about fifty thousand. The *cavea* was divided into five separate zones, called *maeniana*, each designated for specific persons or classes of people. The first *maenianum* consisted of the *podium*, a spacious marble terrace that ran around the upper edges of the protective wall, an area reserved for high-ranking or sacred personages such as the Pontifex Maximus, head priest of the state religion, and the Vestal Virgins, priestesses of the goddess Vesta. On the north side of this platform was the *pulvinar*, or royal box, in which the emperor and his family sat. Opposite them, on the south side of the *podium*, was a box reserved for the Prefect of the City, the public official who oversaw the day-to-day operation of Rome's public works and institutions.

Rising above the *podium* were the other zones: the second, a tier of seats reserved for senators and other distinguished private citizens; the third, for members of the middle class; the fourth, for slaves and foreigners; and the fifth, the *maenianum summum*, consisting of wooden seating installed under a roofed colonnade at the very top of the building, for women. The custom of making women sit farthest away from the arena floor may have originated with Augustus's edict to that effect, designed to shelter them from seeing (and presumably being disturbed at the sight of) the blood and brutality of the spectacles. The very poorest Romans, who had no money to purchase regular seats, were allowed to stand behind the women's bleachers.

Although not a permanent feature of stone or wood, the *velarium*, the giant awning that sometimes covered the amphitheater's open top, was as important to the spectators as their seats. They typically sat watching the games and spectacles for many hours at a stretch. Without protection from the hot Mediterranean sun, this would have resulted in much discomfort, as well as painful sunburns. Raising and lowering the great canopy was accomplished through an ingenious system of ropes, pulleys, and winches. The ropes, which ran over poles jutting from the top of the fourth level to winches located outside the building, formed a spider's weblike lattice across the arena. The lattice held up the individual canvas strips that, when lowered into place one beside another, combined to form the full *velarium*.

The emperor and his family sat in the pulvinar, *shown here behind a modern railing.*

The highly specialized work of operating the *velarium* was entrusted to sailors from Misenum, a naval port on the western Italian coast south of Rome. As scholar Leonardo B. Dal Maso puts it:

> Only sailors who were extremely expert in handling rigging were capable of carrying out such a vast and complex operation, which also required careful training of the greatest precision not only in measuring and placing the various parts of the *velarium* and the machinery, but also in the distribution of the men and their tasks and in their timing. The detachment of 100 sailors from the fleet of Misenum, who lived in barracks near the amphitheater, must have been employed exclusively in the maintenance of the *velarium*; at least a thousand others were needed to raise and lower it and they arrived on ships twice a year.

As the amphitheater's official aerial riggers, these sailors must also have been charged with creating various "special effects" ordered from time to time by the emperor or by the magistrate who organized the spectacles. For instance, Statius, a poet who, like Martial, enjoyed Domitian's patronage, described "the line." This was evidently a rope (or network of ropes) slung across the top of the arena, from which fruit, nuts, and other treats showered down on the delighted spectators. "Scarce was the new dawn stirring," Statius recalled in his *Silvae,*

> when already sweetmeats were raining from the line . . . the famous fruit of Pontic nut-groves, or of Idume's [Palestine's] fertile slopes [probably dates, for which Palestine was famous]. . . . Biscuits and melting pastries, Amerian fruit [apples and pears] not over-ripe, must-cakes, and bursting dates from invisible palms were showering down. . . . Let Jupiter [leader of the gods] send his tempests through the world and threaten the broad fields, while our own Jove [another name for Jupiter, in this case a reference to the emperor] sends us showers like these.

THE LAVISH INAUGURAL FESTIVITIES

The last stages of the great amphitheater's construction— perhaps the colonnade and wooden seating in the extreme upper level, along with various decorative touches—occurred in A.D. 81, during the last few months of Titus's reign and the first few of Domitian's. However, the essential features, including entrances, stone seating, and arena floor, had been completed by the middle of the preceding year. So in the summer of 80, Titus went ahead and inaugurated the building even though it was technically unfinished. It is likely that his haste was motivated in large degree by the golden opportunity to score a large-scale public relations triumph. Earlier that year a serious fire had damaged several sections of the city, and the populace, still disoriented and despondent, needed cheering up.

These opening games, among the most famous (or infamous?) in Roman history, lasted for a hundred days and were extremely lavish and costly. Unfortunately, no detailed day-to-day account of the spectacles has survived; however, fragmentary descriptions by Suetonius, Dio Cassius, and other Roman historians give a general idea of the large scale and diversity of the events staged in the new arena. Apparently, over nine

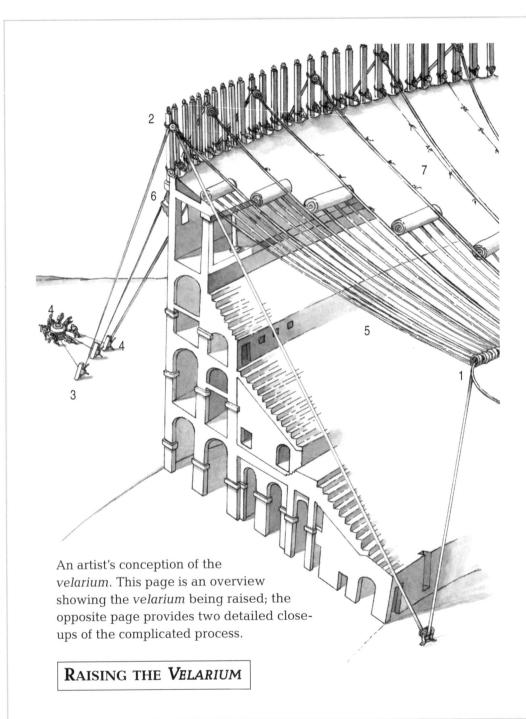

An artist's conception of the *velarium*. This page is an overview showing the *velarium* being raised; the opposite page provides two detailed close-ups of the complicated process.

RAISING THE *VELARIUM*

A ring in the center of the amphitheater (1) is raised by ropes running from the ring to the pulleys on the top level (2) to stone blocks outside (3). Workers turn winches with pulleys (4) on these blocks, raising the ring. There were 160 winches in all outside the building. Each winch was turned by perhaps four to eight sailors, who moved in unison to a pulsating rhythm beaten on a drum or wooden block.

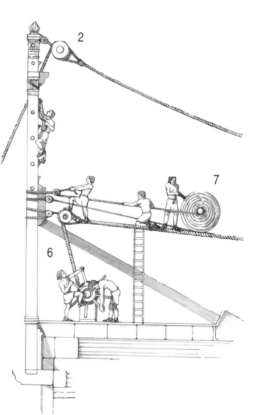

A second series of ropes runs from the underside of the ring (5) to pulleys and winches on the top gallery (6). The strips of the *velarium* (7) are unrolled onto this lower network of ropes, completing the awning. When finally assembled, the *velarium* must have weighed many tons.

THE HUGE JOB OF RAISING THE AWNING

In this excerpt from his book *Rome of the Caesars*, Italian scholar Leonardo B. Dal Maso tells how the sailors from the Roman port of Misenum operated the complex rigging and machinery that moved the Colosseum's huge awning.

The whole apparatus centered on the great ring, like a sort of skylight, to which the ropes holding up the canopy were attached. In the first phase, the ring was raised from the arena [floor level] as far as the level of the cornice [the horizontal roof of the top circular colonnade]: this operation was carried out with ropes which went from the ring to the pulleys at the top of the poles [standing upright on the building's upper perimeter] and from the pulleys to the outside . . . being attached to the 160 large blocks of stone surrounding the amphitheater below. On each of these blocks there was a winch . . . with pulleys for rolling up the ropes. The 160 winches were turned in perfect unison to the beating of time, and this is what raised the ring. When the ring was raised, the ends of the ropes were pulled up and tied to the poles. In the second phase, a second rope was lowered from each of the poles and attached to the ring at a level lower than the first rope: this lower series of ropes, tightened by other pulleys and winches on the terrace of the top gallery . . . formed a sort of spider's web which held up the canvases of the *velarium*. These converging sections were unrolled from above, tied to each other, until they reached the central ring. . . . If all these requirements are taken into account, along with the enormous surface of the *velarium*, the huge weight of the ropes . . . and the static and dynamic problems created by resistance and tension, it must be concluded that raising the canopy was a much more difficult undertaking than erecting an obelisk [a tall, pointed stone structure of enormous weight].

thousand animals of various kinds were slaughtered during the fourteen weeks the games lasted, five thousand of these in a single day! Thousands of gladiators fought and hundreds of condemned criminals met their deaths either by gladiators' swords or the claws and hooves of beasts. As the following account by Dio Cassius informs us, animals fought animals, men (and also women) fought animals, and ships fought ships.

> There was a battle between cranes and also between four elephants; animals both tame and wild were slain. . . . And women (not those of any prominence, however) took part in dispatching them. As for men, several fought in single combat and several groups contended together both in infantry and naval battles. For Titus suddenly filled this same theater with water and brought in horses and bulls and some other domesticated animals that had been taught to behave in the liquid element just as on land. He also brought in people on ships, who engaged in a sea-fight there.

Titus's inaugural festivities were only the beginning of a long tradition of spectacles, some of them colorful and exciting, others brutal and frightening, that the Colosseum would host over the course of ensuing centuries. None of these games and shows were new. They were already widely popular and, some would argue, ingrained in the Roman character long before the foundations for the Flavian arena had been laid. What changed in Titus's reign was the scale of the entertainment and of the violence inherent in it. For the first time, the greatest metropolis in the world had its own permanent and properly immense arena and the shows it featured had to be correspondingly huge. In the coming years many emperors would strive mightily to outdo their predecessors. And some would succeed.

"WE WHO ARE ABOUT TO DIE SALUTE YOU!": LIFE AND DEATH IN THE ARENA

By the time the Flavian emperors erected the Colosseum, the games and shows held there, as well as in the circuses and other public facilities, had already become deeply ingrained social institutions. The Romans collectively referred to large-scale games, shows, and festivals as *ludi*. Some *ludi* were staged to celebrate traditional religious festivals, the *feriae*, such as the *Vestalia*, observed on June 9 to honor Vesta, goddess of the hearth. Other *ludi* evolved as secular festivities, for instance those that honored the memory of important military victories. By the early first century B.C., the Romans observed fifty-seven days of *ludi* and that number continued to grow in the following centuries.

Because much (though not all) work was suspended on these holidays, large numbers of urban Romans were idle for long periods of time. And even during normal workweeks, many Romans were unemployed or dirt poor and consequently could not adequately support themselves. The early emperors recognized the potential danger that if too hungry and idle, the "mob," as the upper classes arrogantly called the common people, might protest, riot, or even rebel.

The solution these leaders adopted and perpetuated was twofold. First, they sponsored regular large-scale distributions of bread and other foodstuffs to the poor. In the Flavian years, as many as 150,000 urban Romans received such handouts at hundreds of distribution centers located across the city. The emperors also spent huge sums subsidizing public festivals, shows, and games.

This policy of appeasing the masses through both free food and entertainment eventually became known as "*panem et circenses*," or "bread and circuses," in reference to a famous sarcastic remark by the first-century A.D. humorist Juvenal. The Roman mob, he said, "limits its anxious longings to two things only—bread, and the games of the circus."

ORIGINS AND TYPES OF GLADIATORS

The *ludi circenses*, or chariot races, to which Juvenal referred, were extremely popular, of course. On each of the approximately seventeen days per year that the Circus Maximus featured these events during the early Empire, people of all walks of life crowded the great racetrack, which sat some 250,000. These crowds were just as eager to attend the *munera*, shows involving gladiators, which were staged in amphitheaters, principally the Colosseum. The number of *ludi* that featured gladiator fights each year is unclear. Like chariot races, the *munera* were very expensive to produce and likely took place only on special occasions and therefore on an irregular basis.

Chariot races in the Circus Maximus were one type of public event designed to keep the masses entertained.

Like so many other customs and ideas, the Romans inherited gladiatorial games from their Italian predecessors, the Etruscans. The Etruscans believed that when an important man died, his spirit required a blood sacrifice to survive in the afterlife (hence the literal translation of *munera*: "offerings"); so outside these individuals' tombs they staged rituals in which warriors fought to the death. In Rome, the *munera* were at first private affairs staged by aristocrats. Over time, however, both they and the general populace came to view these games more as entertainment than funeral ritual, and demand grew for making gladiator fights part of the public games. Julius Caesar was the first leader to stage large-scale public *munera*. According to Suetonius, in 65 B.C. Caesar

The gladiators' barracks at the Colosseum. Gladiators were usually slaves, criminals, or prisoners, but some were volunteers.

put on a gladiatorial show, but had collected so immense a troop of combatants that his terrified political opponents [fearing he might use these warriors against them] rushed a bill through the [legislature], limiting the number of gladiators that anyone might keep in Rome; consequently far fewer pairs fought than had been advertised.

The gladiators who fought in these and later games were mostly prisoners, slaves, and criminals who trained long and hard in special schools; although a few such fighters were paid volunteers. Some of the latter became involved because they were desperate for money, for there was generous prize money for the winners. For others, joining up was motivated by the physical challenge and appeal of danger or the prospect of becoming popular idols and sex symbols who could have their pick of pretty young girls. Among the graffiti slogans still scrawled on Pompeii's walls are: "Caladus, the Thracian, makes all the girls sigh," and "Crescens, the net fighter, holds the hearts of all the girls."

These terms—"Thracian" and "net fighter"—referred to the customary division of gladiators into various types and

GLADIATORS IN THE MOVIES

Unfortunately, few film depictions of ancient Roman gladiatorial combats have been accurately costumed or staged. Two of the notable exceptions were *Demetrius and the Gladiators* (1954, directed by Delmer Davies) and *Spartacus* (1960, directed by Stanley Kubrick). In *Demetrius*, the title character (played by Victor Mature) is a former Greek slave condemned to train at a gladiator school in Rome. At first, because he is a Christian, he refuses to fight. But when one of his friends is apparently killed by a gladiator, he changes his mind. Dressed as a *murmillo*, with crested helmet, short sword, and heavy rectangular shield, he faces and defeats a *retiarius*, armed with net and trident, in an exhibition before the corrupt emperor Caligula (ruled A.D. 37–41) and then goes on to defeat three other opponents simultaneously in an exciting arena battle.

In *Spartacus*, the title character (played by Kirk Douglas) is the real-life slave who led a huge slave rebellion against the Roman state in the first century B.C. Before escaping the gladiator school to which he was brought in chains, he is forced to fight a fellow trainee in a small arena to gratify a group of Roman aristocrats who are visiting the school. Spartacus is arrayed as a Thracian, with an exposed chest, small round shield (*parma*), and curved sword (*sica*), while his opponent is a *retiarius*. Although the latter defeats

Kirk Douglas warily eyes his opponent during combat in a scene from the 1960 movie Spartacus.

Spartacus in the duel, he refuses to slay the fallen man and soon suffers death for his insolence. This scene, like the one in *Demetrius*, impressively recreates the spectacle, excitement, and brutality of the Roman arena.

categories. In this excerpt from his book *The Colosseum*, social historian Peter Quennell describes the four main types that had evolved by the early Empire:

> First came the heavily armed Samnite . . . who carried a sword or a lance and the *scutum*, a [rectangular] shield not unlike . . . [that of] a Roman legionary [soldier]. His chest was naked, but besides his tremendous helmet he wore a protective covering on his right arm and massive armor upon his left leg. Second was the less elaborately armed Thracian, with his *sica*, a curved short sword, and *parma* [small round shield]. Third was the *murmillo*, or fishman, so-called because he had a fish-shaped crest [on his helmet]. He was customarily chosen to engage the fourth class of gladiator, the *retiarius*, or net-wielder. The man with the net was the most lightly armored of all. His face, head, chest, and legs were entirely unprotected. . . . His business was to dart in . . . [entangle] the heavier and clumsier man in his net [and] drive home his massive three-pronged spear.

In addition to the pairings of these main gladiator types, there were a number of special and offbeat types and pairings. These included *equites*, who fought on horseback, and *andabatae*, who grappled blindfolded, as well as archers and warriors who fought from moving chariots. Women gladiators also came into vogue under Nero and Domitian; and Domitian was known to pair women against male dwarves, as well as against one another.

THE ARENA BOUTS AND THEIR OUTCOMES

On the eagerly anticipated day of a gladiatorial spectacle at the Colosseum, the fighters first entered the arena in a colorful parade known as the *pompa*, similar in some ways to the parade of athletes on the opening day of the modern Olympic games. They were usually accompanied by jugglers, acrobats, and other performers, and all kept time to marching music provided by musicians playing trumpets, flutes, drums, and sometimes a large hydraulic organ (the organ probably also played during the actual fighting, producing the same effect as the background musical score of a movie).

At the climax of the *pompa*, the acrobats and other minor performers quickly exited and the gladiators soberly raised their weapons toward the highest-ranking official present. If the emperor was not there, this was usually the *munerarius*, the magistrate in charge of the spectacle. The combatants loudly recited the phrase *"Morituri te salutamus!"* or "We who are about to die salute you!" and at a given signal commenced fighting. The combat was invariably desperate and often savage, and the spectators, like those at modern boxing matches and bullfights, reacted excitedly. Typical shouted phrases included *"Verbera!"* ("Strike!"), *"Habet!"* ("A hit!"), *"Hoc habet!"* ("Now he's done for!"), and *"Ure!"* ("Burn him up!").

This bronze statuette's square shield, sword, and helmet identify it as portraying a Samnite gladiator.

The fighting had several possible outcomes. If both warriors fought bravely and could not best each other, the *munerarius* declared the bout a draw and allowed them to leave the arena and fight another day. When one gladiator went down wounded, he was allowed to raise one finger, a sign of appeal for mercy. The emperor or *munerarius* then made a decision, most often in accordance with the crowd's wishes. If the spectators desired a fighter spared, they either waved their handkerchiefs or pointed their thumbs downward, the signal for the victor to drop his or her sword. At the same time they shouted, *"Mitte!"* ("Spare him!"). On the other hand, if the choice was death, they pressed their thumbs toward their own hearts (symbolizing a sword through the heart) and yelled, *"Iugula!"* ("Cut his throat!").

Another possible outcome was when one fighter killed an opponent outright; and still another was when the fallen combatant pretended to be dead. Few, if any, were successful at this ruse, for men dressed like the Etruscan demon Charun (a retained custom illustrating the games' Etruscan roots) ran out and applied hot irons to the bodies. Any fakers exposed in this way promptly had their throats cut. Then young boys cleaned the bloodstains from the sand and men dressed as the god

Mercury (transporter of the dead) whisked away the corpses, all in preparation for the next round of battles.

OF BEASTS, CRIMINALS, AND CHRISTIANS

The gladiators were not the only popular attractions in the spectacles presented in the Colosseum. There were also ferocious fights between humans and beasts and between beasts and beasts. Noted classical historian Lionel Casson offers this overview of the animal portions of the shows:

> At vast expense the Roman government imported animals from every corner of the known world—tigers from India, leopards from Asia Minor, lions and elephants and other creatures from Africa, wild bulls from northern Europe, and so on. They were kept in cages under the arena until, at the appropriate moment, they were brought up and let loose. As they wandered about, crazed or dazed, *bestiarii*, "beast men," low-level gladiators trained for this sort of thing, stepped in against them with knife and spear; the *bestiarius* had a chance of surviving, the animals none. Or crack native hunters were sent in to cut them down ruthlessly with bow and arrow or javelin—which at least added some dimension of skill to the carnage.

The gruesome toll of animals butchered in this manner must have been enormous. The record of nine thousand beasts slaughtered during the one hundred days of Titus's inauguration of the Colosseum was surpassed in A.D. 107 when the emperor Trajan presented immense spectacles lasting 123 days. At least eleven thousand animals were killed in these games. In the nearly four centuries in which the great amphitheater housed such shows, millions of animals likely met their doom. And all the while, the crowds cheered on the *bestiarii*, who occasionally became almost as popular as winning charioteers and gladiators. Martial left behind this glowing praise for the hunter Carpophorus, who gained fame in the arena during Domitian's reign:

> He plunged his hunter's spear also in a headlong-rushing bear, the king of beasts beneath the cope of Arctic skies; and he laid low a lion, magnificent, of bulk

Animals and humans fight desperately in the Colosseum. Thousands of animals were slaughtered by bestiarii *in shows like this.*

unknown before, one worthy of Hercules' might; and with a far-dealt wound stretched in death a rushing pard [leopard]. He won the prize of honor; yet unbroken still was his strength.

Interspersed with the periodic slaughter of nearly helpless animals were shows featuring the massacre of *completely* helpless humans. While various kinds of petty criminals might be sentenced to the gladiator schools, many of the most serious offenders were condemned to outright execution in the arena. The *munerarius* took charge of these condemned, guaranteeing that each would be killed within a year. Usually at around noon, before the formal gladiatorial bouts had begun, guards herded the unarmed criminals up onto the arena floor, where some were quickly hacked down by a troop of fully armed gladiators. Others were crucified, and still others tied to stakes, on which they were mangled and eaten by half-starved lions, bears, and other beasts.

Some early Christians may have met similar fates in the Colosseum. According to tradition, the first Christian who died in the Flavian Amphitheater was Saint Ignatius, bishop of

Antioch, the first writer to refer to the church as "catholic," or universal. Supposedly, he welcomed martyrdom in the arena and exclaimed shortly before his death, "I am as the grain of the field, and must be ground by the teeth of the lions, that I may become fit for His [God's] table." Although no documented evi-

LAUREOLUS'S GRUESOME PUNISHMENT

The average Roman took capital punishment for granted and found it perfectly acceptable and fitting that murderers and other serious criminals should suffer public execution in the arena. Perhaps the most famous lawbreaker executed before the crowds was the brigand and murderer Laureolus, whose gruesome punishment was the subject of a mime, or short dramatic presentation, composed by the poet Catullus in the first century B.C. Beginning about A.D. 30, actors periodically staged re-creations of Laureolus's execution before crowds in various amphitheaters. In the Colosseum, beginning in Domitian's reign, at the play's climax a condemned criminal took the actor's place and suffered a real execution that was guaranteed to satisfy the most jaded of spectators. The unfortunate individual was nailed to a cross and then, while still alive and conscious, mutilated and eaten by a bear. The popular poet Martial captured the grisly event in one of his famous epigrams (as translated by Walter Ker):

> Laureolus, hanging on no unreal cross, gave up his vitals [insides] defenseless to a Caledonian bear. His mangled limbs lived, though the parts dripped gore, and in all his body was nowhere a body's shape. A punishment deserved at length he won. . . . Accursed, he had outdone the crimes told of by ancient lore; in him that which had been a show before was punishment.

Substitutes for Laureolus continued to die in this same manner in the Colosseum and other amphitheaters across the Empire until at least A.D. 200.

dence exists for Christians dying in the Colosseum, it is probable that hundreds or even thousands were executed there during periodic persecutions of the group in the centuries that followed.

It should be noted that the popular notion that the Romans were religiously intolerant and persecuted the Christians for having different beliefs is mistaken. By Flavian times, the highly tolerant Romans welcomed and themselves practiced dozens of alternative and often exotic religions from around the Mediterranean world, all of which flourished along with the traditional state religion. What made the early Christians different was their own intolerance. In addition to condemning all other beliefs but their own, many of them refused to acknowledge the emperor's authority, which disturbed the traditionally highly patriotic Romans. Moreover, the Christians kept to themselves, appearing to be antisocial, and over time acquired the terrible stigma of having *odium generis humani,* a "hatred for the human race." Worst of all, unfounded rumors spread that Christian rituals included cannibalism, incest, and other repugnant acts. Most Romans came to believe these fables and therefore felt little or no pity for any of the Christians who may have suffered torment and death on the arena's blood-soaked sands.

THE ROMAN FASCINATION FOR GLADIATORS

Yet the spectators who attended the Colosseum and other amphitheaters were not completely pitiless. The frequent modern literary and film depictions of them as cruel and frenzied with blood lust is another common distortion of the Roman character. For one thing, some Romans, particularly the better-educated ones, found the bloodletting of the arena distasteful, even when the participants were hardened criminals. For example, in his *Epistulae morales,* Seneca, the brilliant philosopher and writer who acted as Nero's adviser for some years, expressed his disdain at the slaughter of a group of unarmed condemned men at the noon hour:

> I've happened to drop in upon the midday entertainment of the arena in hope of some milder diversions . . . a touch of relief in which men's eyes may find rest after a glut of human blood. No, no: far from it. . . . Now for butchery pure and simple! The combatants have nothing to protect them; their bodies are utterly open to

every blow; never a thrust but finds its mark. Most people prefer this kind of thing to all other matches. . . . What good is armor? What good swordsmanship? All these things only put off death a little.

The great first-century B.C. politician and orator Cicero had less concern for condemned people receiving "their just rewards," but felt genuine pity for the wholesale killing of animals, who plainly had committed no offense. "There was a kind of compassion," he wrote after witnessing elephants die in the arena, "a feeling that the huge creatures have some sort of fellowship with humans." Sharing these feelings was the second-century A.D. emperor Marcus Aurelius, who thoroughly disliked the butchery of both humans and beasts. Attending the Colosseum strictly out of a sense of duty to his subjects, he ignored the games and utilized the time dictating letters and conducting other state business.

The supremely educated Seneca, Cicero, and Aurelius were undoubtedly in the minority, for most Romans found the arena's spectacles of bloodletting fascinating and entertaining. But before automatically condemning this attitude as cruel and insensitive, one needs to consider that it evolved in a culture with ancient traditions and beliefs very different from our own. The *munera* and wild-beast shows constituted the outward expression of emotions, feelings, and principles deeply ingrained in the Roman character. On the one hand, the Romans had a powerful superstitious awe and fascination for death and all the trappings that accompanied it. In watching other living things die, many experienced a temporary emotional release from their own terror of dying.

On the other hand, Roman fascination with gladiators was bound up in large degree with an obsessive and seemingly contradictory form of hero worship. Socially speaking, gladiators were considered crude, worthless, and undignified lowlifes. Like actors, arena fighters bore the degrading stigma of *infamia*, or "outcast." Yet at the same time, gladiators who won often became popular heroes; and in a gladiator's sacrifice of blood, the Romans perceived a sadly tragic but heroic figure to be admired and honored. The gladiator took a solemn oath that he (or she) would die, without hesitation, for his audience of "betters." Such an act of complete and ultimate submission to the will of one's "master" made the gladiator, in Roman eyes, a model for a person of honor. "There is nothing they [gladiators] put higher than giving satisfaction to their owner or to the people," praised Cicero. Thus, the Romans maintained an odd societal double standard about gladiators. This strongly felt "love-hate" relationship, along with various other deeply rooted religious and ethical traditions and beliefs, made the spectacle of death in the arena highly compelling to Roman audiences.

THE END OF AN ERA

So fascinating were such spectacles, in fact, that they endured, in one form or another, until the end of the Empire in the fifth century. And throughout the intervening years, the Colosseum, universally recognized as the premiere Roman arena, saw almost continuous use. Its great bowl witnessed Trajan's massive games in 107; the appearance of the mad emperor Commodus

A KIND OF COMPASSION

Although the first-century B.C. orator and senator Marcus Tullius Cicero apparently had few qualms about condemned people fighting to the death in the arena, he found the slaughter of helpless animals pitiful and disturbing. In a letter to a friend (translated by W. Glynn Williams in *Letters to His Friends*), he recorded his feelings after attending a *munera*:

Cicero

> Two wild-beast hunts a day for five-days—magnificent, of course. But what possible pleasure can it be to a man of culture when a puny human being is mangled by a tremendously powerful beast, or a splendid beast transfixed [run through] with a spear? And even if it is a spectacle, you've seen it all often, and there was nothing new that I saw. The last day came the elephants—very impressive, but the crowd took no pleasure in them. Indeed, there was a kind of compassion—a feeling that the huge creatures have some sort of fellowship with humans.

as both gladiator and *bestiarius* in the late second century;
and huge wild-animal slaughters to celebrate Rome's one-
thousandth anniversary in the mid-third century.

But toward the close of the fourth century, the nature of the
shows presented in the great amphitheater began to change.
The principal reason was the triumph of Christianity, which,
despite periodic persecutions, had persisted and grown in popularity. Major boosts for the sect occurred in 313, when the emperor Constantine issued an edict granting them religious
freedom, and in 337 when he converted to Christianity on his
deathbed. And a few decades later, the emperor Theodosius
banned the worship of the old Roman gods in favor of the
Christian god. Most Christians viewed the gladiatorial games
as both murder and an offense against humanity. The second-
century A.D. Christian apologist Tertullian harshly denounced
arena spectators, saying:

> He who shudders at the body of a man who died by na-
> ture's law . . . will, in the amphitheater, gaze down with
> most tolerant eyes on the bodies of men mangled, torn

*A statue of a gladiator fighting a lion. The increasing numbers of Chris-
tians in the Roman Empire disapproved of the spectacles in the Colosseum, and the shows' popularity waned.*

to pieces, defiled with their own blood; yes, and he who comes to the spectacle to signify his approval of murder being punished, will have a reluctant gladiator hounded on with lash and rod to do murder.

Though in the Empire's waning years many Romans were still pagans and wanted gladiatorial games to remain, they eventually had to give way to the increasing power of the Christians. By the end of the fourth century, the gladiator schools had been closed, and perhaps about thirty years later, the last actual gladiator fights took place in the Colosseum. In spite of these changes, execution of criminals and beast hunts continued to be held in the arena for at least another century. Surviving writings reveal that as late as 523, half a century after the last Roman emperor, Romulus Augustulus, had been driven from his throne by "barbarian" invaders, the Colosseum still drew huge crowds to watch animal hunts and wrestling matches.

But soon after this period, the city of Rome rapidly declined. Lacking the administration and services the Roman government had provided for so many centuries, it increasingly fell into disrepair and became largely depopulated. By the end of the sixth century, grass had begun to grow on the deserted bleachers where for so long great crowds had loudly cheered and with a turn of their thumbs decreed life or death. The Colosseum's first great era, its years as a working facility, had ended; however, its second and more enduring role, that of a romantic symbol of a lost civilization, was about to begin.

Haunted by the Ghosts of Old Rome: The Colosseum in Later Ages

During most of medieval times, the Colosseum, like much of Rome itself, was a vast ruin that revealed only hints of its former greatness. Although Rome was still inhabited, its population was at best a twentieth of what it had been at the height of the Empire, and the city had degenerated into a decaying, crumbling, poverty-stricken town with little or no central government. As scholar Louise Collis describes it, that town

> consisted of a network of narrow, dark . . . alleyways, broken occasionally by [public] squares, on the flat tongue of land in [a] bend in the Tiber. . . . As one went away from the river, towards the famous seven hills of ancient Rome, one found oneself passing into the country. Sheep and goats grazed among fallen columns and blocks from massive walls.

As for the Colosseum, the *Mirabilia Romae*, or *Marvels of Rome*, a twelfth-century guidebook compiled for religious pilgrims visiting Christian shrines in Rome, passed on the following largely erroneous information (likely confusing the amphitheater with distorted memories of the wonders of Nero's Golden House):

> The Colosseum was the temple of the Sun, of marvelous greatness and beauty, disposed with many diverse vaulted chambers, and all covered with a heaven [dome] of gilded brass, where thunders and lightnings

and glittering fires were made, and where rain was shed through slender tubes. Besides this there were the Signs super-celestial [zodiac signs] and the planets *Sol* and *Luna* . . . drawn along in their proper chariots.

Clearly, by the time these words were written, Italians had forgotten the details of their glorious past, including the original appearance and functions of the Colosseum. This was partly because the building's physical appearance had changed considerably. Large earthquakes had damaged it in the fifth century, in 847, and in 1231, the latter one causing the whole southwestern section of the facade to collapse. And a thick tangle of vines, bushes, and trees had overgrown most of the structure's interior. In their drawings and paintings, medieval artists tried to reconstruct the amphitheater's original form and usually depicted it with a domed covering like the one mentioned in the widely read *Mirabilia*. As time went on, the Colosseum's magnificent remains continued to amaze travelers, like those who had inspired the Venerable Bede, and became a mysterious and romantic symbol of Rome's splendid past.

DEMOLISHING THE LABORS OF THE PAST

But while travelers from the far corners of Europe found the Colosseum's ruins awe inspiring, local Romans increasingly viewed the huge edifice in a practical rather than a romantic

As the centuries passed, the splendor of the Colosseum and the excitement of the events held there faded into obscurity.

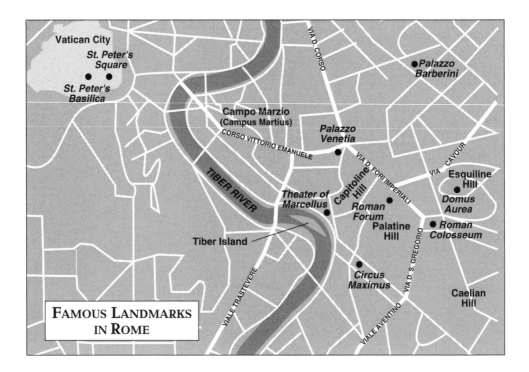

Vatican City
St. Peter's
Square
St. Peter's
Basilica

VIA D. CORSO

Palazzo
Barberini

Campo Marzio
(Campus Martius)

CORSO VITTORIO EMANUELE

Palazzo
Venetia

TIBER RIVER

VIA D. FORI IMPERIALI

VIA CAVOUR

VIA

Esquiline
Hill

Theater of
Marcellus

Capitoline
Hill

Roman
Forum

Domus
Aurea

Palatine
Hill

Roman
Colosseum

Tiber Island

VIA D. S. GREGORIO

VIALE TRASTEVERE

Circus
Maximus

Caelian
Hill

VIALE AVENTINO

FAMOUS LANDMARKS IN ROME

light. After the 1231 earthquake had dislodged and strewn about thousands of travertine stones, the building became a popular source of building materials for newer structures; sadly, out of ignorance for the arena's great historical value, medieval Romans began systematically to demolish their ancestors' majestic labors. The Renaissance pope, Nicholas V (reigned 1447–1455), who established the Vatican library, was said to have removed more than two thousand cartloads of Colosseum stones in a single year. One of his successors, Alexander VI (reigned 1492–1503), went so far as to lease the Colosseum and also the remains of the ancient city's Forum as commercial quarries. Some of the Renaissance structures that bore materials pirated from the great arena were the Palazzo Venezia, Palazzo Barberini, several bridges, and the magnificent Saint Peter's Basilica.

Meanwhile, various popes put what was left of the once-noble Colosseum to some quite ignoble uses. In 1585 Pope Sixtus V (reigned 1585–1590) ordered the architect Domenico Fontana to transform the amphitheater into a textile factory. Fortunately for posterity, when Sixtus died this effort was abandoned. Later, Pope Clement IX (reigned 1667–1669) used the arena as a storage facility for barrels of saltpeter for a nearby gunpowder factory.

It was not until 1744 that the Colosseum's ruins received official government protection. In that year, Pope Benedict XIV (reigned 1740–1758) forbade further removal of stone and other materials from the amphitheater, erecting a monumental cross on the arena floor in memory of the Christians he believed had died there in ancient times. For years to come, standing at a pulpit set up near the cross, poor Capuchin monks delivered sermons to visiting pilgrims.

Yet even Benedict's well-meaning edict protecting the amphitheater did not stop its continuous decay or halt people from further abusing it. Long after the cross had been erected on the arena floor, the seats and terraces of the once gleaming-white *cavea* remained covered by a dense overgrowth of wild olive

AN EXCEEDINGLY GLORIOUS SIGHT

In his *Italian Journey, 1786–1788*, the renowned German writer Johann Wolfgang von Goethe penned the following highly romantic description of his recent visit to the Colosseum:

> Of the beauty of a walk through Rome by moonlight it is impossible to form a conception, without having witnessed it. All single objects are swallowed up by the great masses of light and shade, and nothing but grand and gentle outlines present themselves to the eye. For three several days we have enjoyed to the full the brightest and most glorious nights. Peculiarly beautiful, at such a time, is the Colosseum. At night it is always closed. A hermit dwells in a little shrine within its range, and beggars of all kinds nestle beneath its crumbling arches: the latter had lit a fire on the arena, and a gentle wind bore down the smoke to the ground, so that the lower portion of the ruins was quite hid by it; while, above, the vast walls stood out in deeper darkness before the eye. As we stopped at the gate to contemplate the scene through the iron gratings, the moon shone brightly in the heavens above. Presently the smoke found its way up the sides, and through every chink and opening, while the moon lit it up like a cloud. The sight was exceedingly glorious.

trees, bushes, and grass. Some of the barrel-vaulted corridors became cowsheds and stables, further adding to the mess and ongoing physical deterioration. The sight of such abuse and neglect dismayed James Boswell, the popular Scottish biographer and essayist, when he visited the structure in 1765. "The famous Colosseum," he later wrote, "certainly presents a vast and sublime idea of the grandeur of the ancient Romans." However, he added, "it was shocking to discover several portions of this theater full of dung."

THE AMPHITHEATER BY MOONLIGHT

Boswell was only one of many popular writers from various countries who carried back to their homelands romantic descriptions of Roman monuments, including the ruined amphitheater. Beginning in the 1600s, the Colosseum increasingly

The Colosseum was used as a source of building materials before receiving government protection in 1744.

WILD WEEDS UNDER YOUR FEET

In an 1818 letter to a friend (quoted in Frederick Jones's *The Letters of Percy Bysshe Shelley*), English poet Percy Shelley wrote these words about Rome's colossal amphitheater:

> The Colosseum is unlike any work of human hands I ever saw before. It is of enormous height and circuit, and the arches built of massive stones are piled on one another, and jut into the blue air, shattered into the forms of overhanging rocks. It has been changed by time into an amphitheater of rocky hills overgrown by the wild olive, the myrtle, and the fig tree, and threaded by little paths, which wind among its ruined stairs and immeasurable galleries: the copsewood overshadows you as you wander through its labyrinths [mazes], and the wild weeds of this climate of flowers bloom under your feet. The arena is covered with grass . . . like the skirts of a natural plain . . . the interior is all ruin. I can scarcely believe that when encrusted with Dorian marble and ornamented by columns of Egyptian granite, its effect could have been so sublime and so impressive.

became a prominent image in published diaries, memoirs, and other works by well-known European and American writers. Visiting the arena in November 1644, the influential English diarist John Evelyn recorded:

> We enter into the mighty ruins of the Vespasian Amphitheater, built by that excellent Prince Titus. . . . [It] was once adorned thick with statues, remaining entire [intact] till of late that some of the stones were carried away to repair the City walls, and build the Farnesian Palace. . . . [Inside] is a small chapel called Santa Maria della Pieta nel Coliseo, which is erected on the steps, or stages very lofty . . . and there lives only a melancholy Heremite [hermit]. I ascended to the very top of it, and that with wonderful admiration.

BEAUTIFUL IN ITS DESTRUCTION

In 1832 the popular American landscape painter Thomas Cole visited Rome and was duly impressed by the ancient ruins, particularly those of the Colosseum. In his *Notes at Naples*, he wrote:

> From the great multitude of wondrous things [I saw in Rome], I would select the Colosseum as the object that affected me the most. It is stupendous, yet beautiful in its destruction. . . . He who would see and feel the grandeur of the Colosseum must spend his hour there, at night, when the moon is shedding over it its magic splendor. Let him ascend to its higher terraces, at that pensive time, and gaze down into the abyss, or hang his eye upon the ruinous ridge, where it gleams in the moon-rays, and charges boldly against the deep blue heaven. The mighty spectacle, mysterious and dark, opens beneath the eye more like some awful dream than an earthly reality,—a vision of the valley and shadow of death, rather than the substantial work of man. Could man, indeed, have ministered either to its erection or its ruin? As I mused upon its great circumference, I seemed to be sounding the depths of some volcanic crater, whose fires, long extinguished, have left the ribbed and blasted rocks to the wildflower and the ivy.

The structure also inspired poets, who waxed romantic about both the awesome sight of its remains and the colorful events of its ancient past. One of the first to do so with a fair amount of historical accuracy was Englishman John Dyer, who published his popular *The Ruins of Rome* in 1740. "Amid the towery ruins, huge supreme," he wrote,

The enormous amphitheater behold,
Mountainous pile! o'er whose capricious womb
Pours the broad firmament [sky] its varied light,
While from the central floor the seats ascend

Round above round, slow-widening to the verge,
A circuit vast and high; nor less had held
Imperial Rome and her attendant realms,
When drunk with rule, she will'd the fierce delight,
And op'd [opened] the gloomy caverns, whence rush'd,
Before the innumerable shouting crowd,
The fiery maddened tyrants of the wilds,
Lions and tigers, wolves and elephants,
And desperate men, more fell.

Among the many other famous writers inspired to write about the Colosseum were the English historian Edward Gibbon, who visited its ruins in 1764; German author Johann Wolfgang von Goethe (pronounced GER-ta), in 1786; English poets Lord Byron and Percy Shelley, in 1817 and 1818, respectively; French novelist François Auguste-René de Chateaubriand, in 1828; and American poets Henry Wadsworth Longfellow and Edgar Allan Poe, in 1828 and 1833, respectively. Like many before and after him, Longfellow tried to capture in words the arena's mysterious beauty as it appeared in moonlight:

At length I came to an open space where the arches above had crumbled away, leaving the pavement an unroofed terrace high in the air. From this point, I could see the whole interior of the amphitheater spread out beneath me, half in shadow, half in light, with such soft and indefinite outline that it seemed less an earthly reality than a reflection in the bosom of a lake.

Henry Wadsworth Longfellow

MUTE STONES TELL A PROFOUND TRUTH

The same awesome and romantic qualities that fascinated Evelyn, Shelley, Longfellow, and the others still draw crowds of visitors to the Colosseum. In fact, the great ruined arena, located along modern Rome's Piazzale de Colosseo, a boulevard partly closed to traffic, remains one of the most popular tourist attractions in Europe. Luckily, nearly two centuries of periodic

Nineteenth-century English novelist Charles Dickens wrote that to take in the view from the ruins of the Colosseum was to see "the ghost of old Rome."

restoration have halted and partly reversed the structure's decay. In 1825 workmen set up massive stone buttresses to help keep the surviving sections of the facade from collapsing, and in 1870 all of the vegetation was cleared from the structure's interior. Major restoration efforts occurred from 1893 to 1896, in 1933, and in the mid to late 1970s.

In 1992 the largest such restoration project ever attempted began and is expected to last at least until the year 2002. The minimum goals are to repair and clean existing intact surfaces and to replace the arena floor, which archaeologists removed in the 1800s. One very costly and therefore less definite goal is to move Rome's Metro B subway tunnel, which runs beneath the Colosseum, to a lower position, out of concern that the vibrations from passing trains might cause the structure to weaken and further deteriorate.

In the meantime, parts of the amphitheater, Rome's greatest single architectural symbol, remain open to the public. Visitors are usually admitted free to the lower level, while access to selected sections of the upper levels cost about $3.60 in the mid-1990s, a tremendous bargain considering the magnificent view of the city the uppermost level offers. This is the same view that inspired England's great novelist Charles Dickens to write in 1846:

> To climb into its upper halls, and look down on ruin, ruin, ruin all about it . . . is to see the ghost of old Rome, wicked wonderful old city, haunting the very ground on which its people trod. It is the most impressive, the most stately, the most solemn, grand, majestic, mournful sight conceivable.

Yet as majestic as the Colosseum remains, it is of course but a paltry shell of its former self—the magnificent centerpiece of a great ruling dynasty at the height of one of the greatest and most powerful empires in human history. And in this respect, the amphitheater's cracked stones stand in mute testimony to a profound truth about the fleeting nature of individuals and nations alike. Their crumbling solitude reminds us that no human endeavors or monuments, no matter how splendid and mighty, are ever permanent; in the end, time and circumstance alter and erase them all. As American landscape painter Thomas Cole so aptly put it after his visit to the Colosseum in 1832:

> It was once a crater of human passions; there their terrible fires blazed forth with desolating power. . . . But now all is still [in the ruined arena]. . . . In the morning the warbling of birds makes the quiet air melodious; in the hushed and holy twilight, the low chanting of monkish solemnities soothes the startled ear.

GLOSSARY

agrimensores (or *mensors*): Surveyors; *librators* was another word for surveyors.

amphitheater (in Latin, *amphitheatrum*, meaning "double theater"): A wooden or stone structure, usually oval shaped and open at the top, in which the ancient Romans staged public games and shows, such as gladiator fights.

andabatae: Gladiators who fought blindfolded.

annular: Ringlike; composed of concentric circles.

arcade: A row or continuous succession of arches.

arch: An architectural form, usually curved in a semicircle, used to span the top of a door, window, bridge support, or other open space; the ancient Romans, who inherited the concept from the Etruscans, utilized the arch more frequently, diversely, and inventively than any other people in history.

architrave: A horizontal beam of wood or stone resting atop two or more columns, as in a Greek or Roman temple.

bestiarius (plural, *bestiarii*): "Beast man"; a person trained to hunt and/or fight wild animals in the arena.

Campus Martius: "Field of Mars"; a large open area near the Tiber River in ancient Rome, originally used as a military parade ground, later the site of many important and imposing temples and other public buildings.

canalis: A channel; in Roman architecture, the shallow trough carved in the top of a *chorobates*; if the level of water poured into the trough lined up with the trough's edges, the instrument was properly aligned.

capital: The top section of an architectural column.

cavea: The seating complex of a Roman theater or amphitheater.

chorobates: A wooden device shaped like a bench, used by Roman surveyors to ensure that the ground or a foundation was level.

circus (in Latin, *circensus*): A long wooden or stone structure in which the ancient Romans staged horse and chariot races; the most famous example was the Circus Maximus in Rome.

Corinthian: An architectural order characterized by columns with complex patterns of masonry leaves on the capitals.

cryptoportici: Underground corridors, usually barrel vaults.

Doric: An architectural order characterized by columns with simple, flat capitals.

driver: A chisel with a concave cutting edge, used to cut curves into stone moldings.

equites: Gladiators who fought on horseback.

facade: The outer section, surface, or facing of a building.

feriae: Traditional religious festivals and holidays in ancient Rome.

gouge: A chisel with a cutting edge shaped in a right angle, used for cutting perfect corners into stone sculptures.

infamia: Socially outcast, as in the case of Roman actors and gladiators.

Ionic: An architectural order characterized by columns with scroll-shaped volutes on the capitals.

keystone: The central, topmost voussoir in an arch.

kivel (or stonemason's ax): A tool having a head with a vertical cutting edge on one side and a horizontal edge on the other, used for cutting blocks of stone; the dual head allowed the mason to make both vertical and horizontal cuts without having constantly to change position.

ledgers: In Roman scaffolding, the horizontal planks running parallel to the wall in front of which the scaffolding was erected; the workers stood on the ledgers.

ludi: Large-scale public games, shows, and festivals in ancient Rome.

ludi circenses: Chariot races.

maeniana (singular, *maenianum*): Separate seating zones in the *cavea* of a Roman amphitheater.

maenianum summum*:* In a Roman amphitheater, the uppermost seating tier, containing wooden bleachers set aside for women spectators.

Morituri te salutamus!*:* "We who are about to die salute you!"; the phrase recited by gladiators just prior to combat.

mortarium*:* A wooden trough in which Roman masons mixed mortar.

munera*:* "Offerings"; private or public gladiatorial shows.

munerarius*:* The magistrate, or public official, in charge of the *munera*.

murmillo*:* "Fishman"; a kind of gladiator, heavily armored and carrying a sword and rectangular shield, whose massive helmet bore a fish-shaped crest.

odium generis humani*:* "Hatred for the human race"; the attitude mistakenly attributed by the Romans to the early Christians.

panem et circenses*:* "Bread and circuses"; the Roman government policy of distributing free food to the urban masses while heavily subsidizing the public games and shows.

parma*:* A small round shield used by Thracian warriors and gladiators.

pier: A vertical support for an arch.

pilaster: A rectangular ornamented column, usually set partway into a wall.

podium*:* A flat marble terrace running around the lower portion of the *cavea* in a Roman amphitheater; a seating section reserved for royalty or high-ranking officials.

pompa*:* The paradelike ceremony that opened a Roman gladiatorial spectacle.

Pontifex Maximus: "Chief pontiff"; the head priest of ancient Rome's state religion.

pulvinar: "Royal box"; in an amphitheater, the seating section reserved for the emperor and his family.

pulvis Puteolanus: The mortar used in making Roman concrete; named after the town of Puteoli, near Mount Vesuvius, the main source of the volcanic sand that constituted its main ingredient.

punch: A tool, resembling a long railroad spike, that a worker struck with a hammer to cut or make indentations in blocks of stone.

putlogs (or putlocks): In Roman scaffolding, the horizontal supports running at right angles to the wall in front of which the scaffolding was erected; sometimes the inner ends of the putlogs were inserted into "sockets," or holes, in the wall in order to give extra support.

radial: Projecting outward from the center, as the spokes of a wheel.

retiarius (plural, *retiarii*): "Net-wielder"; a kind of gladiator who wore no armor and carried a net and a long trident.

Samnite: A member of a fierce central Italian hill tribe conquered by the Romans during the early Republic; or a kind of gladiator attired as a Samnite warrior—heavily armored and carrying a sword and rectangular shield.

scabbling hammer: A tool resembling a pick, used for cutting and shaping blocks of stone.

scutum: The large rectangular shield carried by Roman soldiers and also by certain gladiators, including the *murmillos* and Samnites.

sica: A curved short sword wielded by Thracian warriors and gladiators.

spectacula: "Place for spectacles"; the term used to describe early arenas, such as the one at Pompeii, before the term amphitheater had been coined.

stagnum: An artificial pond; the Colosseum was built on the site of the *stagnum Neronis*, the small lake the emperor Nero installed on the grounds of his infamous Golden House.

standards: The vertical supports in the wooden scaffolding used by Roman builders.

Thracians (in Latin, *Thraces*): Natives of the northern Greek region of Thrace; or gladiators attired as Thracian warriors—lightly armored and carrying a curved sword and small round shield.

travertine: A durable, finely textured, creamy-white variety of limestone, frequently used in Roman construction.

tufa: A lightweight stone composed of compressed volcanic ash, used extensively in Roman buildings.

vault: An elaboration or extension of an arch into three dimensions; in essence, a curved ceiling; like the arch, the vault, particularly the barrel vault, a corridor or tunnel with a curved roof running along its length, became a trademark of Roman construction.

velarium: A huge awning spread across the open space at the top of a Roman theater or amphitheater to shield the spectators from the sun.

volute: A spiral- or scroll-shaped decoration on the capital of an Ionic column.

vomitoria (singular, *vomitorium*): Entranceways in ancient Roman buildings.

voussoir: One of several individual wedge-shaped elements that form the curve of an arch.

For Further Reading

Ian Andrews, *Pompeii*. Cambridge, England: Cambridge University Press, 1978.

Isaac Asimov, *The Roman Empire*. Boston: Houghton Mifflin, 1967.

Editors of Time-Life Books, *Pompeii: The Vanished City*. Alexandria, VA: Time-Life Books, 1992.

L. A. Hamey and J. A. Hamey, *The Roman Engineers*. Cambridge, England: Cambridge University Press, 1981.

Anthony Marks and Graham Tingay, *The Romans*. London: Usborne Publishing, 1990.

Susan McKeever, *Ancient Rome*. London: Dorling Kindersley, 1995.

Claude Moatti, *In Search of Ancient Rome*. New York: Harry N. Abrams, 1993.

Don Nardo, *The Roman Empire*. San Diego: Lucent Books, 1994.

———, *Greek and Roman Theater*. San Diego: Lucent Books, 1995.

———, *Life in Ancient Rome*. San Diego: Lucent Books, 1996.

———, *The Age of Augustus*. San Diego: Lucent Books, 1996.

WORKS CONSULTED

ANCIENT SOURCES

Cicero, *Letters to Atticus* (in three volumes). Translated by E. O. Winstedt. Cambridge, MA: Harvard University Press, 1961.

————, *Letters to His Friends* (in three volumes). Translated by W. Glynn Williams. Cambridge, MA: Harvard University Press, 1927–1929.

Dio Cassius, *Roman History*. Translated by Earnest Cary. Cambridge, MA: Harvard University Press, 1927.

Sextus Julius Frontinus, *The Stratagems and the Aqueducts of Rome*. Translated by C. E. Bennett. Cambridge, MA: Harvard University Press, 1925.

Juvenal, *Satires*, in *Latin Literature in Translation*. Edited by Kevin Guinagh and Alfred Paul Dorjahn. New York: Longman's Green and Company, 1952.

————, *Satires*, published as *The Sixteen Satires*. Translated by Peter Green. New York: Penguin, 1974.

Martial, *Epigrams* (in two volumes). Translated by Walter C. A. Ker. Cambridge, MA: Harvard University Press, 1919–1920.

————, *Epigrams*, in *The Epigrams of Martial*. Edited and translated by James Mitchie. New York: Random House, 1972.

Pliny the Elder, *Natural History* (in ten volumes). Translated by H. Rackham. Cambridge, MA: Harvard University Press, 1967.

Pliny the Younger, *Letters*, in *Pliny: Letters and Panegyricus*. Translated by Betty Radice. Cambridge, MA: Harvard University Press, 1969.

Statius, *Works* (in two volumes). Translated by J. H. Mozley. Cambridge, MA: Harvard University Press, 1961.

Suetonius, *Lives of the Twelve Caesars*, published as *The Twelve Caesars*. Translated by Robert Graves and revised by Michael Grant. New York: Penguin, 1979.

Tacitus, *The Annals*, published as *The Annals of Ancient Rome*. Translated by Michael Grant. New York: Penguin, 1989.

————, *The Histories*. Translated by Kenneth Wellesley. New York: Penguin, 1993.

Vitruvius, *On Architecture* (in two volumes). Translated by Frank Granger. Cambridge, MA: Harvard University Press, 1962.

Modern Sources

Jean-Pierre Adam, *Roman Building: Materials and Techniques*. Translated by Anthony Mathews. Bloomington: Indiana University Press, 1994.

Thomas Ashby, *The Aqueducts of Ancient Rome*. London: Oxford University Press, 1935.

J. P. V. D. Balsdon, *Life and Leisure in Ancient Rome*. New York: McGraw-Hill, 1969.

Carlin A. Barton, *The Sorrow of the Ancient Romans: The Gladiator and the Monster*. Princeton: Princeton University Press, 1993.

Matthew Bunson, *A Dictionary of the Roman Empire*. New York: Oxford University Press, 1995.

L. Sprague de Camp, *The Ancient Engineers*. New York: Ballantine Books, 1963.

Jerome Carcopino, *Daily Life in Ancient Rome: The People and the City at the Height of the Empire*. New Haven: Yale University Press, originally published 1940, new edition 1992.

Lionel Casson, *Daily Life in Ancient Rome*. New York: American Heritage Publishing, 1975.

Raymond Chevallier, *Roman Roads*. Translated by N. H. Field. Berkeley: University of California Press, 1976.

Louise Collis, *Memoirs of a Medieval Woman*. New York: Harper and Row, 1964.

Tim Cornell and John Matthews, *Atlas of the Roman World*. New York: Facts On File, 1982.

F. R. Cowell, *Life in Ancient Rome*. New York: G. P. Putnam's Sons, 1961.

Leonardo B. Dal Maso, *Rome of the Caesars*. Translated by Michael Hollingworth. Rome: Bonechi-Edizioni, n.d.g.

James K. Finch, *Engineering and Western Civilization*. New York: McGraw-Hill, 1951.

Johann Wolfgang von Goethe, *Italian Journey, 1786–1788*. Translated by W. H. Auden and Elizabeth Mayer. New York: Pantheon Books, 1962.

Michael Grant, *The Gladiators*. New York: Delacorte Press, 1967.

———, *The World of Rome*. New York: New American Library, 1960.

L. A. Hamey and J. A. Hamey, *The Roman Engineers*. Cambridge, England: Cambridge University Press, 1981.

Edith Hamilton, *The Roman Way to Western Civilization*. New York: W. W. Norton, 1932.

Frederick L. Jones, ed., *The Letters of Percy Bysshe Shelley* (in two volumes). Oxford, England: Clarendon Press, 1964.

Richard S. Kirby et al., *Engineering in History*. New York: McGraw-Hill, 1956.

Senatore R. Lanciani, *Ancient and Modern Rome*. New York: Cooper Square Publishers, 1963.

William L. MacDonald, *The Architecture of the Roman Empire*. New Haven: Yale University Press, 1982.

Claude Moatti, *In Search of Ancient Rome*. New York: Harry N. Abrams, 1993.

Colin O'Connor, *Roman Bridges*. Cambridge, England: Cambridge University Press, 1993.

Peter Quennell, *The Colosseum*. New York: Newsweek Book Division, 1971.

Betty Radice, *Who's Who in the Ancient World*. New York: Penguin, 1973.

Chris Scarre, *Chronicle of the Roman Emperors*. London: Thames and Hudson, 1995.

Jon Solomon, *The Ancient World in the Cinema*. New York: A. S. Barnes and Company, 1978.

Hans Straub, *A History of Civil Engineering*. London: L. Hill, 1952.

J. B. Ward-Perkins, *Roman Imperial Architecture*. New York: Penguin Books, 1981.

Mortimer Wheeler, *Roman Art and Architecture*. London: Thames and Hudson, 1964.

L. P. Wilkinson, *The Roman Experience*. Lanham, MD: University Press of America, 1974.

INDEX

93

Picture Credits

About the Author

Classical historian and award-winning writer Don Nardo has published over seventy books. In addition to this volume on the Colosseum, his studies of ancient Rome include: *The Roman Empire, Life in Ancient Rome, The Age of Augustus, Caesar's Conquest of Gaul, The Punic Wars*, a biography of Julius Caesar, and others. Of his many books about ancient Greece, his forthcoming *Philip and Alexander: The Unification of Greece* is the only modern study written for young adults offering a detailed account of the exploits of Philip of Macedonia. Mr. Nardo also writes screenplays and teleplays and composes music. He lives with his wife, Christine, on Cape Cod, Massachusetts.

$22.45

DATE			